heritage

A Father's Influence
to the Generations

WITH STUDY GUIDE

TOM LANE

GATEWAY®
PRESS

ISBN: 978-1-945529-39-9 Paperback
ISBN: 978-1-945529-40-5 eBook
ISBN: 978-1-945529-41-2 Spanish

We hope you hear from the Holy Spirit and receive God's richest blessings from this
book by Gateway Press. We want to provide the highest quality resources that take the
messages, music, and media of Gateway Church to the world. For more information
on other resources from Gateway Publishing, go to gatewaypublishing.com.

Gateway Press, an imprint of Gateway Publishing
700 Blessed Way
Southlake, Texas 76092
gatewaypublishing.com

21 22 23 24 25 — 5 4 3 2

This book is dedicated to my father, James Mitchell Lane; to my grandfathers, Harry Mitchell Lane and Newell A. Zuspan; and to my father-in-law, Dean Russell Frazier. The heritage of these fathers and their influence on my life continues to bless future generations through my children, grandchildren, and all who are benefited by this book. The influence of a father cannot be overestimated!

Contents

Foreword by Jimmy Evans   xi

Foreword by Todd Lane   xiii

Acknowledgments   xvii

Introduction   xxi

Section One
Establishing Standards

1. Taking a Personal Inventory   3
2. Understanding the Nature of Your Child   15
3. Influencing Your Children Toward Godliness   31
4. Developing a Healthy Fear of
   God in Your Children   51

Section Two
Transferring Standards

5. A Matter of Character   79
6. Faith's Influence on Character Development   101

7. Components of Balanced Discipline
   Part 1—Submission 115
8. Components of Balanced Discipline
   Part 2—Correction 133
9. Components of Balanced Discipline
   Part 3—Accountability 151
10. Using the Experiences of Life
    as Your Classroom 167

Section Three
Supporting Standards

11. The Importance of Spending Time
    with Your Children 189
12. The Balance of Two Perspectives 205
13. Preparing Children for Their Destiny 215
14. Raising Righteous Teenagers 227
15. Helping Teenagers Handle Social Pressure 241

Section Four
Protecting Standards

16. Responding to Wayward Children 259
17. Partnering with God through Prayer 281
18. Establishing Your Legacy 295

Study Guide

How to Use the Study Guide 321
Introduction and Chapter 1 323

Chapters 2-4   327

Chapters 5-6   331

Chapters 7-10   335

Chapters 11-15   339

Chapters 16-17   343

Chapter 18   349

About the Author   353

Foreword

I have known Tom Lane for over thirty years as my close personal friend and work associate. Without a doubt, he is the best father I know and has more authority to write a book on how to be a successful father than anyone I have ever known. His four children are living testimonies to his ability to use his influence as a father to raise terrific kids.

I have learned a great deal from Tom over the years in how to be a better parent. When I met him, I was in my mid-twenties, and my children were very young. In watching Tom father his children, I was challenged and changed. My life and my children's lives have been deeply blessed by his example.

I encouraged Tom to write this book because of his obvious understanding of the subject and the great need that exists for men to learn to be good fathers. Many men in our society today have never had a father's influence in their lives and therefore don't know what to do or how to do it in fathering their own children. Others have had negative examples from their own fathers and need to overcome past hurts and learn positive parenting skills.

Whatever category you fall into, I highly recommend this book. In fact, I believe every mother would benefit from reading it also. Even though the subject is male-oriented, these pages are filled with rich parenting skills that transcend gender.

Tom Lane is a great father. He has influenced my life in a profound way. I am grateful to God for putting him in my path as my dear friend, and I am thankful for this book that will touch all of us with Tom's rich insights on how to be a successful father.

Jimmy Evans
Best-Selling Author
Founder of MarriageToday

Foreword

I became a father in the year 2000. My wife, Blynda, and I were living in Auckland, New Zealand, where I was on a two-year work contract. It was there we had our first child, Olivia. My parents came to visit their new grandchild, and while on that trip, my dad began writing this book.

Dad would write a chapter and then read it to my mom, Blynda, and me. As I listened to him read his thoughts, it occurred to me how consistent and true this man is. Every word is accurate, authentic, and absolutely real to who he is and how he lives his life. Not one time did I think, "Yeah, that sounds more like something you would have liked to happen, but it didn't really go that way." No, the truth of his life is written in every word. Every word reflects the man I knew growing up, the man I knew as he wrote the book, and the man I know today.

I don't know anyone like my dad. He is so pure of heart that his innocence actually gets him in trouble sometimes. (Those are stories for another book!) He is so consistent that the entire church knows where he eats breakfast every day. He is so humble that he lives a life submitted to leaders around him. He is so servant-hearted that there is absolutely nothing he wouldn't do for someone in need. As a gifted leader, he's helped birth, grow, and establish two mega-churches. I have had countless people tell me that my dad is like a father to them, even though many of them are actually older than him!

When this book first came out, my siblings and I joked that we made our dad the man he is today—you know, with all the incredible opportunities we gave him to develop his fathering chops! What we truly appreciate, though, is that we were blessed with a one of a kind father. We have watched our dad lead our family with humility, grace, and servanthood. The influence of our father has truly shaped our lives. This book is filled with our stories, and we can guarantee that our dad speaks with actions way more than words. Every word you read is supported by real actions that we experienced.

Blynda and I added two more children to our family—Harrison in 2003 and Evelyn in 2006. I suppose the greatest challenge facing any new father is, like most experiences, the fear of the unknown. Is there a greater responsibility than shaping the course of a human life? I think not. A child's future is a blank canvas. While anyone will be the product of his or her own choices and experiences, the unique role of a father to lead a developing child through the turbulence of life is a calling of the highest order. Today, as a father of two teenagers and one pre-teen, I am in the thick of this thing called fathering. I had the best teacher, and I pray that God uses this book to capture your heart and encourage you to be the greatest influence you can be as a father or mother.

As the oldest child in the Lane family, I am the lucky one who gets to write this foreword. But I do so on behalf of my siblings (Lisa, Tyler, and Lindsay); our spouses (Blynda, Braxton Corley, Marci, and Brett Huckins); and the 15 grandchildren (Olivia, Harrison, and Evelyn; Lane, Christian, and Slade; Amelia, Caroline, William, and James; Harper, Henry, Hazelle, Holland, and Hunter).

Much love,
Todd Lane

P.S. Don't be confused. This book has everything to do with our Mom, too!

Acknowledgments

T his book would not have come about without the encouragement and support of my best friend, Jimmy Evans. Over the years, he has identified gifts in me and called them out, sometimes having to overcome my own resistance. I am forever blessed because of our friendship; it is a special gift from God that I do not take for granted. Thank you, Jimmy!

As I have written this book, my wife and children have been constant sources of encouragement and support. I especially thank Jan for more than 45 years of love and commitment. She is my friend and partner, and without her, there would be no stories to tell and no children to influence. Jan, you are the most wonderful gift God has given to me!

I want to thank Todd, Lisa, Tyler, and Lindsay for allowing me to share our experiences. I am blessed by your love, and I am overjoyed to see your responses to God and His hand directing and blessing your lives. I have been overwhelmed with joy as I have watched you select your mates and begin your families. I am thankful for God's hand on your lives and for the way you are raising your children. God's word is true!

Jan and I now have the perspective of four generations of God's loving kindness to celebrate and reflect upon. Praise God!

There are many people who have contributed immeasurably to the completion of this project and its printings. Thanks to my friends at Majestic Media and Trinity Fellowship Church who helped make the original printing of this book possible. Thank you to Gateway Church and Gateway Publishing for their work to make the reprints and updated versions possible.

A special thanks to all my associates at Marriage Today for their hard work and commitment to the family. Working with this ministry for more than 23 years has been an honor and a privilege. Finally, thanks to Ken Gire for his thoughtful consideration of my draft and his wise and experienced counsel on the original printing of this book.

I would be remiss if I did not give thanks to the elders and congregation of Trinity Fellowship Church who have loved me and allowed the structure of ministry to accomplish great things for God, including their extension of ministry through Gateway Church and my involvement there these last 14 years. I appreciate the relationship that Trinity Fellowship Church and Gateway Church hold in ministering together, and I am thankful for the support of the Gateway Church Elders and congregation as this effort to help men and women become the influence God has ordained for them continues in His master plan.

Introduction

The Heritage of a Father:
The Gift That Keeps on Giving

Accomplishments and material things are temporary at best.
Measure your success in life by the heritage you leave
your children.

" I never knew the extent of God's love for me until I was
44 years old," a man once told me. He had not understood God's love because it had not been properly represented in his childhood home or reflected in his relationship
with his father. This man is fortunate to have overcome this
deficit so that a new cycle of blessing can be established in
his family as he reveals God's love to his children.

As a pastor, I have discovered that most people are
unaware of how much influence their father's presence
or absence has had on them, whether negative or
positive. To be a successful father, a man must have a
pattern to follow—a model to copy. He must have been
fathered successfully or have another source from which
to be trained. Sadly, our society offers very few solid
resources in this area.

For those seeking answers, there is an ominous "black hole" when it comes to instructions about fatherhood. Popular parenting books offer alternative methods that seek to fill the instruction void; unfortunately, many recommend lifestyles that do not consider God. God's method is time-tested, and its results are proven to bring blessings to families and changes to nations.

There are others more academically qualified to speak to the issues of child development. My purpose in writing this book is to share my childhood and family experiences and how they have shaped my life. It is out of these experiences that I came to know God, and through knowledge of Him, I formed my parenting philosophies. I am a father of four children, all now adults. My family is an intact family. My parents were married over 40 years. My dad was a great dad, and he imparted fathering skills that I have applied to the parenting of my own children. My story is not one of "my kids went to hell, and this is how I got them back." Mine is a story of faithfulness—God's faithfulness to me and my faithfulness to Him.

I have sought to love God and serve Him with my whole heart and to influence my children to do the same. This book tells how my father, grandfathers, and father-in-law influenced my life and how I took their influence and coupled it with my love for God to train and prepare my children for life. I pray that by sharing my experiences and the principles I have learned, families will be strengthened and fathers will become effective in their God-ordained call to lead and influence their children.

A boy needs a father to train him in godly character and responsibilities. He needs a model to prepare him for his own role as a father. Likewise, a girl needs guidance to know what to expect from a man in his role as her husband and the father of her children. She needs to see the model first in her own father.

God's plan calls for children to be trained in the home and to pass their knowledge from generation to generation. In fact, over the last 6,000 years, God's plan has been available through His prophets and teachers, and His plan is still available to mankind through the Bible.

The social ills we are currently experiencing have their roots in our failure as fathers. It is clear to me that a father's influence cannot be overestimated as it relates to forming character, transferring values, and leading children into dynamic personal relationships with God.

It is clear to me that a father's influence cannot be overestimated as it relates to forming character, transferring values, and leading children into dynamic personal relationships with God.

My life is a testimony of the power of the positive influence of a father. I am fortunate to have fond memories of my childhood. Simply stated, my dad was a great father. His presence was an influential factor in my development as a man. From his father, he learned and incorporated for himself the direction, discipline, and affirming attention necessary to provide the foundation for a stable home. As his father had done with him, my dad demonstrated love to me with hugs, consistent positive behavior, and words of affirmation.

I am his product, and I have incorporated his model into my parenting philosophy, which is anchored in the belief that "Children are a gift from the Lord" (Psalm 127:3). What we model and transfer to our children through our behavior must be a reflection of God and His plans for our life and theirs. As such, we must approach fatherhood with the same diligence as the builders of the Empire State building. We must lay a solid foundation. We must consistently add bricks of truth and character with the utmost care and integrity. Most importantly, we must build as God, the Master architect, intended.

In the pages ahead, I provide practical information and instructions for men who want to be influential fathers to their children and leave a lasting legacy for them. **Legacy** can be visualized as a seesaw. On one end is **inheritance**—this includes *tangible* resources such as money, property, and possessions. On the other end

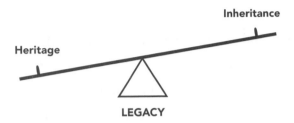

is **heritage**—this includes *intangible* resources such as character, values, and beliefs.

Inheritance and heritage are both important, but does one outweigh the other in eternal significance? Perhaps you have the ability to leave great wealth, fancy cars, and exotic vacation homes to your children. Perhaps your estate is more modest. Either way, remember this— tangible resources, though meaningful, are *temporary*. They may last a long time, but they won't last forever. If you want to leave an eternal legacy for your children and future generations, you must impart a godly heritage. But how does this work?

The cornerstone of my parenting philosophy is the principle of *transference*—the idea that we will transfer to our children the values and character demonstrated in our own lives. In other words, our values must be modeled by our own behavior if we want them to transfer to our children. Transference forms the hub around which all other issues of parenting influence revolve. When we understand this principle, we realize that our actions are a much more influential tutor than the instruction of our words or the concepts we believe but do not practice.

Using the principle of transference, I have set out to lead and influence my children (Todd, Lisa, Tyler, and Lindsay), with the full expectation that they will pass onto their children the values I have modeled and molded into them. This system of influence is the method God intends parents to use as they build and prepare the next generation.

Through thirty-plus years of pastoral counseling experience, I have come to understand that not everyone has as fond memories of childhood as I do. Many suffered from abandonment, violence, and abuse. Others suffered from neglect, the result of fathers who were distracted or disinterested. Many men also suffered from a lack of biblical training in the household. Tragically, this flow of hurt and dysfunction continues and multiplies from one generation to the next.

Whatever your background, I want you to know it is never too late to start. Perhaps you are overwhelmed at the responsibility of being a father. Perhaps you are paralyzed by fear because you have little or no training for fatherhood. This fear is quite common. Fortunately, God specializes in rewarding latecomers. In Matthew, Jesus tells the parable of a vineyard owner who pays each of his workers the same amount, even though some did not work as long or as hard as the others. When faced with complaints, the vineyard owner simply replies, "I wish to give to this last man *the same* as to you" (Matthew 20:14).

No doubt it is best to understand your role as a father before you have children. However, even if it is late in your parenting day and even if your children are grown or almost grown, the good news is that you can still implement God's principles. As you implement them, God becomes a partner in your efforts to become the best father possible.

Your parenting story may not resemble mine. However, if you are looking for a way to call your children back from potentially tragic situations, the principles discussed in this book will give you tools to help. Regardless of your current situation, your efforts to learn and apply God's principles will produce good fruit and blessings for your children.

God has given men the high calling of *fatherhood.* Greater than any business exploit or ministry success, with the power to accomplish more than any man's fortune, is the potential influence a father has to a thousand generations (Exodus 20:6). It is worth the effort to learn and apply God's principles to our own lives so that through the principle of transference, we can become influential fathers to our children and our children's children. In doing so, you can experience God's blessings on your family through multiple generations.

Scripture is true when it states, "Your lovingkindness is better than life" (Psalm 63:3). I hope you will find much value in the chapters ahead and apply what you read for the benefit of your family and your influence as a father.

God's promises are real. His blessings are eternal. It is never too late to start.

Section One

Establishing Standards

1

Taking a Personal Inventory

You must have a personal relationship with
God to be able to transfer it to your children!

After teaching a course about God, a university professor made a startling discovery. On the first day of class, he had asked his students to answer questions (in writing) about their relationships with their fathers—*How does your father exact discipline? How does your father express his love to you? What actions on your part make your father proud? What actions disappoint your father?*

At the semester's end, after months of biblical teaching about God's attributes and His unfailing love for mankind, the professor again asked his students to answer questions. These questions were similar to the first set but with a twist. This time the subject was God—*How do you believe that God exacts discipline? How does God express His love to you? What actions on your part make God proud? What actions disappoint God?*

Upon comparison, the professor discovered that his students' perceptions of God were direct reflections of their relationships with their fathers! What is the moral of this story? A father's influence determines his child's view of God more than a whole semester of in-depth study of biblical truths!

Although not scientifically proven, I submit that the results of this informal poll ring true. To be successful fathers, we must demonstrate God's nature to our children. We cannot simply shift the responsibility to our spouses, Sunday school teachers, or other people of influence in our children's lives. We must have a day of reckoning to accept for ourselves the fact that as fathers, we have a profound influence on the outcome of future generations.

A father's influence has a ripple effect. Like a stone thrown into a pond, our influence produces ripples that impact our sons and daughters, washing over them and circling ever larger across future generations. These ripples affect every area of our children's lives: friend-ships, education, marriage, personal and professional accomplishments, finances, and most importantly, where they will spend eternity.

Our goal should not merely be to bring up politically correct children who become religious adults and fit well into society. *Rather, our goal should be to rear children who understand how uniquely important they are in the eternal scheme of things and who comprehend that true satisfaction in life is only found in recognition of God's deliberate work and purpose.*

Accomplishing this is not a shallow religious act, nor is it a duty of good citizenship, as if the transfer of knowledge forms the basis of fulfillment and purpose. It must be our goal to transfer to our children a dynamic relationship with the living God who created us and loves us. The transfer of this relationship happens through the personal involvement of a father's heart and soul and is reflected in the total commitment of his being.

> *It must be our goal to transfer to our children a dynamic relationship with the living God who created us and loves us.*

To lay the foundation for a relationship with God in our children, we first must understand two foundational truths:

1. God is the Creator and owner of all things.
2. Man's purpose and destiny are only fully found in service and surrender to Him.

Only with a complete understanding of these truths can we effectively represent God's nature to our children.

God is the Creator and Owner of All Things

On January 22, 1973, the United States Supreme Court made a fundamentally flawed decision that unleashed gigantic and tragic waves of immorality across our country. The case was Roe vs. Wade, in which the high court legalized abortion on demand. This decision resulted in the elimination of greater numbers of people than the six million Jews systematically murdered during the Holocaust in World War II. Since 1973, approximately 59 million abortions have been performed in the United States. According to the United States Census Bureau, this number is more than triple the population of America's five largest cities combined in 2010.

The court's premise for this decision was that human sexual activity in itself produces a pregnancy. It further concluded that sexuality is under the sole control of the individuals participating in the sexual act. On this logic, the court ruled that it is a woman's right to decide the outcome of her pregnancy.

The flaw in this reasoning is exposed in the Bible's clear portrayal of God as the Creator who works in the womb to form us. It is clear that birth is not an accident. God's hand guides the biological process of conception so that each person is the product of His will and work. *Life is God's determination, not woman's choice.* This is evident in the fact that even with a world population exceeding 7.5 billion, every single person's fingerprints are different (on each finger no less!) and completely formed in the womb in the sixth month. Each one of us is unique, a product of God's design.

> For You formed my inward parts;
> You covered me in my mother's womb ...
> My frame was not hidden from You,
> When I was made in secret,
> *And* skillfully wrought in the lowest parts of the earth.
> Your eyes saw my substance, being yet unformed.
> And in Your book they all were written,
> The days fashioned for me,
> When as yet *there were* none of them
> (Psalm 139:13, 15–16).

> Your hands have made me and fashioned me,
> An intricate unity (Job 10:8).

> "Before I formed you in the womb I knew you;
> Before you were born I sanctified you;
> And I ordained you a prophet to the nations"
> (Jeremiah 1:5).

God knows every person's weaknesses, and He factors them into His divine plans. When God called Moses to lead the children of Israel out of Egypt, Moses objected, citing slow speech as his reason. God answered, "Who has made man's mouth? Or who makes the mute, the deaf, the seeing, or the blind? *Have* not I, the LORD?" (Exodus 4:11).

God is the Creator of all things, and the Bible tells us that all things were created by Him to fulfill His purposes. Colossians 1:16 says:

> For by Him all things were created that are in heaven and that are on earth, visible and invisible, whether thrones or dominions or principalities or powers. All things were created through Him and for Him.

In treating birth as a right of human choice, the Supreme Court erred. The court failed to acknowledge that God is the Creator of everything, and as His creation, mankind is ultimately accountable to Him. The Supreme Court is not supreme. God created all things, animate and inanimate; therefore, He is the rightful owner of all creation, and we are responsible to Him for our actions.

God created all things, animate and inanimate; therefore, He is the rightful owner of all creation, and we are responsible to Him for our actions.

Understanding these foundational truths should radically sharpen a father's view of his parenting role.

Suddenly, he realizes that procreation is God-centered, not human-centered. Life is a gift. God divinely initiates conception, guides development in the womb, and entrusts the gift of life to us!

Man's Purpose and Destiny Are Only Found in Service and Surrender to God

An awareness of God has always been part of my life. He was discussed at our dinner table. He was honored on Sundays. And although I could not see Him, my parents and grandparents demonstrated through their lives that God was a real person, very much alive and a central part of our home.

My family attended church out of gratitude toward God, not out of fear that failure to acknowledge Him might evoke His wrath. We regarded the Bible as worthy of lifelong study and considered it a privilege to gain greater knowledge of God and His ways. We prayed regularly, humbling ourselves in service to Him. We freely gave time and money to the church, helping others with no expectation of acknowledgment or reward. Love for God was the reason—not benevolence, humanitarian service, or social etiquette.

My parents set an example of having a living, breathing relationship with a Supreme Being. Naturally, almost effortlessly, they transferred this concept to me—not only in words but also by consistent actions. Their example served as the foundation for a very important decision I made at age 16. At that point in my life, God became more than a religious concept to me. He used circumstances to break through my insensitivity, and suddenly, I was aware of Him. I knew He was there, and it was more than an awareness of religious knowledge or tradition as I'd had before. I understood that He was offering me a one-on-one relationship with Him. Fortunately, my father, (future) father-in-law, and my grandfathers had shown me the way. They did not see the pursuit of God as something only for preachers, women, children, and the elderly. Instead, they led by example, and their leadership made it easy for me to surrender my life to Jesus Christ. Through my personal act of surrender, God became alive and real to me. More than a concept, He became my friend, Savior, and Lord.

Without my father's influence, I might live as many men today, viewing God only in religious terms or perhaps not viewing Him at all. Currently, there exists a mindset that "real" men do not need God. Many of today's men see God as a weakness and a crutch, rather than the Supreme Creator who is the source of true power and success. A father will not be fully effective as a leader and teacher to his children without acknowledging God in the entire process of life. *Proper values and character in their truest and purest forms are only found in God.* Apart from Him, the values and character we try to transfer either become diluted or do not transfer at all. The teaching and training we give to our children will never measure up if we say, "Follow me. I know the way—I alone am the model." If we remove God from our parenting, we will miss the mark in developing our children to their fullest potential.

> *A father will not be fully effective as a leader and teacher to his children without acknowledging God in the entire process of life.*

Many fathers already understand that their model was not a good one, but they mistakenly believe they have nothing else to offer. And yet, no father wants to tell his son, "Do not live like me. Be like your friend's father." I believe every father's heart desires to leave a meaningful heritage of his beliefs, values, and standards that will enable his children to experience overflowing measures of fulfillment, purpose, and destiny.

We must first take inventory of our lives. The principle of transference reminds us that we cannot transfer to our children what we do not have. It only makes sense to begin with our own relationship with God as we consider how to raise our children.

A Concluding Thought

Based on the discussion in this chapter, I hope you agree with me and recognize that God created our children with unique gifts to fulfill His plan. He created them, and they belong to Him, but they have been entrusted to us to be developed to their full potential and purpose through our influence. We cannot introduce our children to God and help them discover His plan for their lives without knowing Him ourselves. *We must have a personal relationship with God to be able to transfer it to our children!*

Where are you today? Is God a religious concept? Or is He an important part of your life, as demonstrated daily through a living relationship?

The author of Hebrews tells us, "For he who comes to God must believe that He is, and *that* He is a rewarder of those who diligently seek Him" (Hebrews 11:6). In other words, a person must first believe that God exists and, secondly, that God promises to reward those who make a steady, earnest effort to find Him.

And what is the reward? Romans 6:23 says, "For the wages of sin *is* death, but the gift of God *is* eternal life in Christ Jesus our Lord."

The reward of diligently seeking God is finding abundant life, in this world as well as in eternity. Abundant life is found only through God's Son, Jesus Christ—"I am the way, the truth, and the life. No one comes to the Father except through Me" (John 14:6).

We cannot work our way to God with charitable deeds (Romans 3:23). We cannot serve our way to Him through religious dedication (Titus 3:5). We can only come to Him through an acknowledgment that our best efforts to be good and please Him have failed. By doing so, we agree with Him, opening the door to accept His offer of forgiveness.

This is the gospel: Jesus Christ died for us so that we might have restoration, forgiveness, abundant spiritual life, and intimacy with God. When we accept this truth, God becomes more than a concept. He becomes real and walks with us each day. As a result, He enables us to live as positive role models for our children, leading them in the footsteps of Christ.

Every person will make one of two decisions in life: accept Jesus Christ as Lord and Savior and receive the benefits of a relationship with Him or reject His offer of relationship and choose to live by self-fashioned rules. The rejection of Jesus brings its own penalty and sabotages the influence God intends fathers to have on their children.

I encourage you to be bold and accept Christ today. He is the true source of power and success. This is the single most important decision you will ever make. The influence of a father begins with the decision to be influenced by the truth of God in a personal way. Do not wait; act now.

The Bible says, "For with the heart one believes unto righteousness, and with the mouth confession is made unto salvation" (Romans 10:10). Pray this life-changing prayer out loud:

> *Jesus, I confess that I am a sinner. All my efforts to be good and please You have failed. I thank You that You paid the price for my sins. I ask You to forgive me, come into my life, and make me new inside. With Your daily help, I will follow You for the rest of my life. Amen.*

As you spoke the prayer above and surrendered your life to Christ, you received the gift of salvation! The step you have taken will allow God to change you and develop His character and values in your life. He will empower you to live for Him and enable you to transfer His work in your life to your children. *You will become the father of influence God created you to be!*

2

Understanding the Nature of Your Child

As precious and unique as each child is, we must not forget
that there is foolishness bound up in his or her little heart.

Foolish acts make no sense to the logical mind. They lack forethought, wisdom, and appropriate measures of caution. Every person I see in counseling wants his or her actions to be evaluated based on the intent behind the actions, rather than the results. Rarely is the same grace extended when evaluating others' actions. Adults relate this way in their relationships, and when they become parents, they relate this way to their children. Even though we'd like to be judged by our intentions, we often become frustrated and impatient when we catch our children in some act of foolishness. We ignore their intent and focus on their behavior.

Wise fathers understand that their children will do things that make no sense, lack forethought, and have no measure of wisdom or caution associated with them. The foolish behavior of our children is an opportunity to discover their intent and teach our values. By our reactions, we can show them how to use forethought and draw on their own experiences or the wisdom of others before acting.

The foolish behavior of our children is an opportunity to discover their intent and teach our values.

The Bible is very clear on this matter. It tells us to expect children to act foolishly, to not be surprised by their foolish behavior. When faced with our children's foolishness, we must diligently train them and lovingly correct their foolish actions.

Every one of us could tell stories of the childish, foolish, or even stupid things we have done. Foolishness is not a respecter of personality, social class, ethnicity, or religious belief, nor is it a respecter of authors who write books on fatherhood.

It was the summer of 1960 in Omaha, Nebraska. In the middle of a long, hot day, I was *bored*. Homework and the rigid schedule of third grade were long forgotten. I needed excitement, something different to break up the monotony.

Then it hit me: I would build something! In the garage, I searched the scrap pile for wood and my dad's workbench for tools. I couldn't find his regular claw hammer, so I grabbed the next best thing—his ball peen hammer, a funny-looking tool with a fat, rounded end designed for shaping metal or pounding out dents.

I set up shop on the front porch, a four-foot square slab of concrete just the right size for this eight-year-old to hammer and saw and nail. I don't remember what I set out to build; I just remember that I was excited to have everything I needed.

Eagerly, I cut several boards and started nailing them together with the ball peen hammer. I had hammered several nails into the boards when one of the swings went awry, missed the nail, and ricocheted off the board. With cat-like reflexes, my foot jerked out of the way of the uncontrolled hammer as it knocked a circular chunk from the porch's front edge. Suddenly, all interest in the construction project left me. I was mesmerized by the hammer's work on the edge of the concrete porch.

For the next half hour, I centered my attention on the porch, knocking out concrete chunks to create a jagged edge and then tapping each to make it uniform. The creative genius of my work was intoxicating.

Down the street, one of my friends saw me hammering away, and he walked over for a closer look. He examined the litter of broken concrete and the jagged porch, and he asked me, "What are you doing?!"

I was brought to the full awareness of my foolishness as I explained how I got started knocking chunks off the edge of the porch. I went flush when my friend exclaimed, "When your dad gets home, he is gonna kill you!"

First, reality set in; then panic. There I stood in a mixture of awe and terror, struggling to find a way to undo my destructive work.

To my surprise, my dad did not ground me for life or give me something more physically impressionable to underscore his displeasure. To be sure, he was disappointed and frustrated. He asked for an explanation: "*What* were you thinking?"

"I don't know-w-w!" My voice had turned into the whine of a child caught in a foolish act.

Nevertheless, although well aware of the expense to fix a broken porch, my dad did not focus on the cost of my action. It would have been easy for him to lecture me on the stupidity of my behavior. I'm sure it must have been tempting to rub my nose in the fact that my actions had absolutely no forethought. And due to my lack of caution, I failed to consider the consequences of my behavior. My dad would have felt justified in administering a painful punishment to teach me the lesson of my life—one that I would never forget.

To this day, I am still amazed he did not raise his voice as he talked to me about my stunt. He did not have to convince me of the foolishness of my behavior. Instead, he made me walk through the steps of repairing the porch. As I became aware of all that was involved in fixing the damage, I realized the consequences of my foolishness. Although the cost of the repair was well beyond my ability to pay, my dad saw to it that I made some level of restitution by sacrificing my allowance and some of my savings. He fit the punishment to my maturity level and the sacrifice to my age and ability.

Even as adults, there are times when despite our best efforts to avoid foolishness, it finds us. A common problem for many adults is exceeding the speed limit while driving. When a police officer approaches our car window and declares his radar clocked our car going over the limit, he asks, "Is there an emergency?" We hear ourselves ramble some empty excuse, and suddenly what made perfect sense just a few minutes earlier no longer does. Even chiding ourselves with personal rebukes ("You should know better!") does not solve the dilemma created by our foolishness as adults, nor will it properly correct our children's foolish behavior.

Our children's potential is in our hands as it relates to taming negative instincts and cultivating positive virtues within them. This is the reality of responsible parenting. No father can succeed without understanding the capacity for foolishness common to all men. A successful father is one who can correct foolish behavior without inflicting emotional hurt. Accomplishing this is like mastering any other skill; it is not difficult, but it does require practice.

> *A successful father is one who can correct foolish behavior without inflicting emotional hurt.*

Corrective discipline is the means to address the foolish nature in our children. *The purpose of discipline is always redemptive.* God does not intend for it to be abusive, destructive, or harsh. Loving concern for the development of the child should motivate all discipline.

A father's proactive and positive response to the foolish behavior of his child determines whether the correction will produce the desired result. If his response is uncaring, negative, or rejecting, the child's foolish nature will go unchecked, leading to a life of behavioral dysfunction. This dysfunction will not be outgrown but will produce unhealthy fruit as the child moves into adulthood.

In Chapter 7, I offer specific steps to help you accomplish the positive work of discipline in your children. For now, let me say that for these steps to be effective, we must avoid three common tendencies:

Don't Reject the Child Along with the Behavior

Men often respond to foolishness with verbal and physical abuse—doing and saying things that scar children for life, such as labeling them as "stupid" or "failures." *A father's lashing out to instill fear in his children does not scare away foolishness.* In fact, quite the opposite happens. The foolish nature embeds even deeper, leaving children with scars of rejection.

When a child's foolish nature appears in some action or behavior, a father should never express dissatisfaction through rejection. Neither should we expect a child's foolish nature simply to evaporate without the diligent care of corrective discipline. A successful father gives loving acceptance to his children while correcting the foolishness of their behavior.

Every father must realize that God gives him a naturally foolish child at birth. Proverbs 22:15 begins, "Foolishness is bound up in the heart of a child."

However, children also have tremendous God-given potential, unique to them. Sometimes a child's silliness is so cute, we can't help but laugh; other times, it is expensive (as in the cost of repairing a jagged concrete porch). Often, it is extremely frustrating. Whether cute, expensive, or frustrating, we must realize that our attitude and the discipline we administer will determine whether a child overcomes his or her natural foolishness.

Foolishness is not about knowledge, I.Q., or genetics. It is about the sin nature common to man. Regardless of intellect, ability, or personality, we are all infected with the curse of a naturally rebellious and foolish nature, which began with Adam and Eve's fall (Genesis 3). This nature struggles with the wonderful virtues of God imparted to us through the instruction of our parents. It is critical for parents to correct the foolishness that is the seedbed for sin in their children and cultivate the character of God and His virtues so that His nature prevails in their children's natural attitudes.

As an answer to foolishness, the conclusion of Proverbs 22:15 says, "The rod of correction will drive it far from him." This wisdom expressed by Solomon brings understanding to our children's negative behavior so that we can deal with it positively. God's solution for subduing sin and promoting righteousness is wise, caring parents who understand the true nature of their children and respond with loving discipline.

I look back with great admiration upon my father and his handling of the broken porch incident. To this foolishness many fathers may have responded improperly, perhaps with abusive words, harsh punishment, or rejection. My father corrected me for my foolishness, but he was aware that foolish actions are part of the training process between a father and his children. To this day, I bear the lasting fruit of my father's loving influence and positive correction to my many acts of childhood foolishness.

Don't Delegate the Discipline

Fathers often delegate discipline to mothers or someone else. As a counselor, I frequently hear this excuse: "I am gone all day at work. I don't want to be the heavy when I get home."

When a man sees the role of the disciplinarian as "the heavy," it is usually because this is the way his father administered discipline. The man recoils from these negative childhood experiences and, as an adult, removes himself from similar situations with his own children. This response opens the door to fear—the paralyzing fear of becoming verbally or physically abusive. Due to the power of their personalities or physical strength, men often convince themselves that someone gentler and less physical should administer correction.

In reality, nothing could be further from the truth. God has established fathers as the doorkeepers of the home. Whatever a father tolerates will be tolerated; whatever he resists will be systematically rooted out. Notice how Ephesians 6:4 specifically addresses fathers:

*Whatever a father tolerates will be
tolerated; whatever he resists
will be systematically rooted out.*

And you, fathers, do not provoke your children to
wrath, but bring them up in the training and admonition
of the Lord.

Men are to be the initiators of discipline and teaching
in the home. This isn't to say that women aren't equal to
men or that they are less important in the development
of children. It is to say that the Bible commands the
father to lead. A father must support and reinforce the
discipline administered by the mother. Unity between
husband and wife is a necessary factor for correction to
be fully effective.

If a father delegates the responsibility to the mother
but she is passive or refuses to administer discipline, the
negative effect is compounded in the children. In this
case, the foolish behavior is never addressed, leaving
the child to self-develop. The results are dysfunctional
behavior patterns, which affect every area of life—all
because the father won't apply the biblical mandate and
bring correction to the foolish nature of his child.

I watched a young man in our church self-develop
like this. His dad was a hard-working man whose job
took him away from home many weeks. However, he
always attempted to be home on the weekends. In his

early teens, the young boy was taller and stronger than his mother, and although she tried to correct him when he got out of line, she had no means of enforcement. When her husband was in town on the weekends, he did not want to strain his relationship with his kids by enforcing correction, so he did not discipline his son. His wife could not administer the discipline she knew was necessary because her son was just too big.

This young man struggled with authority at school and could not keep a job. The wrong crowd of friends influenced his behavior, and this grieved his mom and dad. Although they did not agree with what he was doing, they failed to correct his behavior, and he was left to self-develop. As a young adult now, he lacks purpose and direction, and he continues to lead a life dominated by foolish behavior.

Every woman I know loves for her husband to be proactive in their children's lives. When women are released from the unfair burden of "doing the dirty work" of discipline, a beautiful thing happens: security, freedom, and love emerge in the marriage, and children become the "peaceable fruits of righteousness," as stated in Hebrews 12:11:

> Now no chastening seems to be joyful for the present, but painful; nevertheless, afterward it yields the peaceable fruit of righteousness to those who have been trained by it.

Don't Project Unrealistic Expectations

Men learn through experience that to succeed, you must produce results. This pressure to produce often leads to self-imposed standards of performance and unrealistic expectations in their lives. It also can be the catalyst for unrealistic expectations of perfection to be placed upon their children. When this happens, the result is long-term emotional damage.

As adults, we do not hold up under the pressure of these expectations, and neither do our children. Correcting foolishness is a process. No potter expects instant results from his lump of clay; he establishes the desired end result in his mind's eye and skillfully crafts his piece of clay into the work he envisions. Likewise, a father must establish the vision and values that will govern the activities of his home. Through patient and skillful work, he carefully molds his vision and values into the lives of his children, producing a treasure for God.

My friend, Jimmy Evans, tells the story of counseling a man who lacked confidence in new situations. He was paralyzed by the fear of failure. As they worked to discover the source of this man's fear, the man very reluctantly revealed a situation of hurt from his childhood. When this man was eight years old, he went to the garage to be with his dad who was doing repair work on the family car. He stood beside the car listening and watching while his dad worked underneath. His dad called out to him to get the crescent wrench off his workbench. The young boy did not know what a crescent wrench was, so he took a guess and grabbed a random tool. When he handed it to his dad, his dad threw it across the garage and yelled at him, calling him stupid and cursing him for not getting the right tool. His dad finally ended the verbal tirade with, "If you don't know any more than this, get out of my garage and go help your mother in the house where you belong."

The man was devastated by his father's words and his own inability to live up to his father's expectations. The scar of this event stuck with him through his growing up years and was replayed in his adult mind as he encountered new situations. His insecurity and fear were linked to this experience. He never again wanted to endure the rejection he had received from his father, so he felt trapped and unable to approach new situations with confidence.

How else is a boy to be taught, if not by involvement with a father who has realistic expectations for his student? A father's role is not that of a resident potentate to be served by a crew of servant children. Instead, a father must be a trainer, equipper, motivator, mentor, and coach. A father must have compassion, vision, patience, and steadfast commitment to the process of preparing and molding his child's life with positive and corrective reinforcement.

As a trainer, he imparts to his children the fundamentals of behavior. As an equipper, he prepares his children for service by providing the necessary resources. As a motivator, he inspires and challenges his children to achieve what is thought to be impossible. As a mentor, he shows his children the way by highlighting the principles that apply to each situation, having himself walked the path of preparation. As a coach, he evaluates the progress, correcting his children through positive interactions when they miss the mark.

There is no higher purpose for a father than to develop the full potential of his children so that their lives are immersed in love and service to God.

A Concluding Thought

I believe God has been with you as you have read the pages of this chapter. Through the gentle work of His presence, I believe He has been making specific application of this material to you, personalizing it through situations in your own family.

Are you frustrated by your children's imperfections? Have you shifted the burden of correction to your wife or someone else? Do you resent your children's foolish behavior or perhaps harbor unrealistic expectations about their development apart from your careful and patient input? Are you realizing, perhaps for the first time, that parenting is a process?

These are tough questions to ask and even tougher ones to answer.

The Bible tells us that imperfection is woven into the human fabric, to be removed only through proper correction over time. The remedy begins with an understanding of the nature of children and continues with a commitment to the corrective process. Removing unrealistic expectations and accepting your responsibility to provide vision, values, and discipline for your children empowers them to step into God's perfect plan for their lives. This is the guarantee for God's blessing now and in the future.

Why not be honest with God today and acknowledge your need for His help? James 1:5 says, "If any of you lacks wisdom, let him ask of God, who gives to all liberally and without reproach, and it will be given to him." The phrase "without reproach" means without mocking, ridiculing, or using angry or sarcastic words. God is merciful and gives wisdom without reminding us of our unworthiness.

Why not acknowledge any areas of shortcoming and initiate a discussion with your wife regarding the changes necessary in you and your family? When two are in agreement, God is released to do His most miraculous work.

Although foolishness is part of a child's nature,
correction will drive it far away and, in the process,
will produce a beautiful treasure for God! It takes a
diligent, faith-filled father, partnering with his wife, to
lead the effort and produce the result I am describing.
This partnership will produce the fullest results in your
children. Why not work with your spouse to apply the
principles we have discussed in this chapter? The results
will not come quickly, but they will be awesome!

3

Influencing Your Children
Toward Godliness

Children are influenced more by the life parents model
for them than by words, good intentions,
or any other factor of influence.

A uthor Thomas Carruthers once said, "A teacher
is one who makes himself progressively unnecessary." So it is with successful parents—their daily
guidance and oversight become unnecessary as they
skillfully transfer their values and beliefs to their
children.

In this chapter, I offer practical insights and tools into
making the transfer of godliness and moral character
a natural part of your family life. By presenting my
solutions to some commonly shared parenting struggles,
my experiences can work to your advantage. As Thomas
Edison said, "I have not failed; I've just found 10,000
ways that won't work." He made this statement on his
way to inventing one of the greatest innovations ever to
benefit man: the light bulb.

Before we talk about methods, we must first ask ourselves, "What am I trying to transfer?" We can only transfer those things that we possess, whether physical or spiritual. *Our children will only accept from us what we actively experience and model in our lives.* So, let's take an honest look at ourselves and ask some pointed questions.

First, define your relationship with God. Is it personal and intimate? Impersonal and religious? Formal and works-oriented? Legalistic and rules-centered? An impersonal relationship with God produces a life void of spiritual vibrancy. God's values are time-honored and unchanging. They are not based on what seems right in given situations. When God created man, He established a relational system designed to impart His values to mankind. God's values are still worthy of being embraced in our lives today. The single most important value we can transfer to our children is a loving commitment to God their Creator.

Second, ask yourself if you have the kind of relationship with God you want to transfer to your children. In other words, do you want your children to grow up to be like you in spiritual commitment, consistency, and character? Remember, you can only transfer those things you possess. If you do not possess a vibrant, personal relationship with the Lord, you should make some changes to assure that you transfer the proper spiritual understanding and experiences to your children.

We must honestly examine ourselves before we can concentrate on who we want our children to become. We must ask ourselves, "Does my example support or conflict with the proper model for my children to copy?" Only when we are positive examples of what we are trying to transfer into their lives will our children understand and accept what we have to say.

In recognizing the importance of this concept, we discover one of the keys to successful parenting: *children are influenced more by the life parents model for them than by words, good intentions, or any other factor of influence.* Therefore, the first consideration in any endeavor to "shape" our children must be to create a standard: a positive example fashioned from our own lives to serve as the reference point and pattern to follow.

We must be shaped first. Only then can we deal with the secondary but all-important question of how to choose the best methods of transferring the convictions and practices of our lives to our children. Hopefully, you have done a self-review while reading this section, and now you are ready to consider the godliness of your children.

Four Specific Times to Transfer Godliness

Long ago, my wife, Jan, and I individually committed to personal, vibrant relationships with God. Our decisions served as spiritual "insulation" from lifeless practices of religious obligations, bland ceremonies, and pious procedures. We also committed to an all-out effort to transfer our vibrant, personal, and active relationships with the Lord to our children. The question was: How do we accomplish this?

Jan and I had established personal quiet times dedicated to Bible study and prayer early in our lives. Our effort to establish this in our family proved difficult. Our children's ages varied so widely that it was hard to keep everyone's attention. Soon, the time became a boring obligation that everyone dreaded, which defeated the entire purpose. The results were consistently disappointing.

But out of our disappointment, we discovered a better way. The book of Deuteronomy tells of a training method that is practical, powerful, and relationally dynamic. It is the extreme opposite and a welcome relief from a dry, religious program. God's instruction for parents comes through Moses with these words:

> "And these words which I command you today shall be in your heart. You shall teach them diligently to your children, and shall talk of them when you sit in your house, when you walk by the way, when you lie down, and when you rise up" (Deuteronomy 6:6–7).

God tells us to train our children throughout the day as natural opportunities arise. There are four specific times mentioned:

1. When we *sit in our house*, or as we enjoy home life
2. When we *walk by the way*, which today translates "to travel by car, plane, etc."
3. When we *lie down*, or get ready for bed
4. When we *rise up*, or as we prepare to start the day

It is a lifestyle of seizing the moment throughout the day. Daily circumstances become potential classrooms for teaching children to apply faith and other principles of godliness. This method is dynamic, practical, and personal. It tailors the training to children's unique personalities and experiences. More importantly, it is the only method I found that truly produced spiritual vibrancy in my children.

> *Daily circumstances become potential classrooms for teaching children to apply faith and other principles of godliness.*

When I grew up, my family did not have devotions. We talked about God and regularly attended church, but there was no family devotion time. My understanding and training about God came from church. When I was 13, I went through communicants class so that I could join the church. It was dull, boring, and

religious—it was lifeless! Through this experience, I
developed the idea that God is something important
that we make part of our life on Sunday, but He has
little practical benefit or effect the other days of the
week. My perception was based on my experience at
home and in the church.

However, when I met Jesus in a personal way, I
realized the concept of God formed by my experiences
was not right. I definitely did not want to transfer this
false concept to my children, and I did not want them to
have this perception to overcome as they pursued and
developed relationships with God. It is this type of false
perception that creates religious experiences but not
dynamic followers of Jesus Christ.

I am not against family devotions. If they produce
good results for your family, use them. When they no
longer produce the results you want, look for other
creative ways to impart God's love and relationship
to your children. Regardless of your method, here are
several guidelines to help you make the transfer a
success.

Walk the Walk—Don't Simply Talk the Talk

Children possess a wonderful ability to see through
deception and pretense. With kids, if you say it, you
better mean it, and more importantly, you better

be doing it. For instance, if we as parents do not set the example of carving time for God out of our busy days, then how can we advise our children to do so? Children have their own pressures in life with school, work, friends, sports, etc. Our solution will carry no authority if we have not first solved this dilemma for ourselves. We must lead by example, or the transfer will fail! Instruction, as the saying goes, is more caught than taught.

I talked with a father who was concerned and frustrated by his son's inability to control his temper. It was most notable when he competed in sporting events. His son would vent his frustration with demonstrations of anger toward himself, other players, his coach, the refs, and sometimes even spectators. This young man was a polite and pleasant person to be around until he became frustrated by his performance in competition or by the perceived injustice of a decision that did not go his way. Although his father was diligent to correct his son's outbursts, the correction seemed to have no lasting ability to change his son's behavior. As we talked, I agreed with the father's corrective response to his son's behavior, and I was puzzled by its lack of effectiveness—until I played basketball with the father in a pick-up game. His behavior was the same as his son's during the heat of competition. I finally understood why his correction was not working with his son. His behavior was a much stronger influence than his words of correction. *We cannot expect our children to do what we say if we are not able to do it ourselves.* Our instruction will not transfer.

Never Waste an Opportunity

Teaching opportunities usually have two things in common: they are unexpected, and they are inconvenient. When they come, we must take advantage of them because they may never be recreated quite the same way.

Bedtime is a prime teaching time for young children. They seem to be the most talkative and inquisitive just before going to bed. When this happened with my children, it was tempting to label their behavior as a charade, an attempt to delay going to sleep as long as possible. A wise parent, however, uses discernment to evaluate the teaching opportunity of every moment and uses it to its fullest advantage.

My dad looked for teaching moments throughout the day, at what seemed to be the strangest times. As my family enjoyed casual conversations during dinner, my dad would suddenly turn to one of my sisters or me and say, "Do you know that I love your mother?"

My immediate thought was, "Uh oh, here it comes. Dad's on his soapbox again."

When he asked this, my sisters and I knew he was addressing all of us. "Yes, Dad," we would say in unison.

"Do you know that she was here before you?"

"Yes, Dad."

He would make eye contact with each of us. "Do you know that she is going to be here after you're grown and gone?"

Our chorus was labored and weary. "Yes, Dad."

"So, don't try to get between your mom and me," he would say.

The final "Yes, Dad" would finish the dialogue, and we would move onto another subject. It was painless and somewhat corny, but it etched one of my father's important values into our lives.

Good teachers sometimes resort to corny methods to impart a principle. As a child, you may have been turned off or even embarrassed by a "corny" lesson, yet later you retrieved the important principle or concept. What adult did not learn the alphabet by singing the little ditty "A-B-C-D-E-F-G" as a child, only to recall it under his breath years later as he tries to put a list of objects in alphabetical order?

The method may have been corny, but the truth of the lesson stuck. In his corniness, my dad taught us about his commitment to our mom and to their marriage. He declared their unity, along with establishing the reality that his relationship with her had priority in our family. He also exposed the manipulative tendency of children to play one parent against the other. We knew that our dad's relationship with our mom was a priority, and we never even tried to get between them or manipulate them.

In word and deed, my father imparted important values. He wanted his children to understand and adopt his pattern of priority, commitment, and unity as it related to marriage. He was a wise teacher who knew that he must impart and enforce his values at every opportunity. He knew that simply yelling when we did something wrong or only teaching us during times of crisis would not work.

If my dad had only attempted to teach us his values when he was correcting our wrong behavior, his efforts would have failed. This is where many fathers make mistakes. The primary time for training and imparting values is not while administering correction or at the point of frustration. We *reinforce* our values through correction, but we *impart* our values most effectively by seizing teachable moments as they arise in normal circumstances throughout the day. Therefore, influential fathering is a full-time responsibility and requires the wise use of every opportunity and situation as a backdrop to illustrate and impart godly values and character.

We reinforce our values through correction, but we impart our values most effectively by seizing teachable moments as they arise in normal circumstances throughout the day.

Be Consistent In Your Behavior and the Modeling of Your Values

Nothing is more confusing for a child than inconsistently applied instructions. Parents must remember that a child thinks in concrete terms and does not understand relative or abstract concepts. Thus, a child cannot make sense of a parent who verbally stresses the importance of going to church and yet attends one week and misses three.

To be influential fathers, we must make some tough decisions and commitments. Is telling the truth *always* the right thing to do, or is it optional when confronted by a police officer or the I.R.S.? Is wholesome language important all the time or only when your pastor is in the room? Do adults and children have the same moral parameters, or do adults have the right to exclude certain standards?

Early in life, Jan and I made a moral decision against drinking alcohol for reasons more fully explained in Chapter 15. We, of course, understand that not every

Christian will reach the same conclusion we did, but we discussed our values regarding alcohol and the reasons behind them with each of our children as they reached their teen years. Our motive was to help them decide their position on alcohol for themselves.

Throughout life, every person will have to make moral decisions that affect his or her behavior. As parents, it is our responsibility to ensure our actions are consistent with the values represented by our decisions. Otherwise, our influence over our children is diminished, and our values do not transfer.

My dad was a smoker, much to the concern of my mom and each of us kids. We were concerned for health reasons and were thrilled when he stopped smoking at sixty years old. As a child, I suffered from asthma, and my dad would often tell me, "I smoke, but you shouldn't because you have asthma"—as if his concern for my health was more important than our concern for his own. Once again, the principle of transference comes into play. In this instance, my dad failed to realize that his behavior had to be consistent with the value he held for it to transfer. Just having a conversation about his fatherly concern would not transfer the value he was trying to impart! My dad's input did not influence my decision on smoking because he was talking to me about a value he did not model through his behavior.

Jan and I have been careful to watch for and eliminate inconsistent behaviors in our lives as we point them out in our children's lives. One of these inconsistent value situations came up the summer after our eldest son, Todd, had graduated high school. He landed a job in the pro shop of a local golf course. One weekend, the golf course hosted a big tournament, and one of the largest sponsors was the area beer distributor. On the final night of the tournament, Todd brought home a souvenir: a large, plastic beer bottle that had served as a tee marker for the tournament.

He presented it to Jan and me with fanfare, his face flush with excitement. "Isn't it cool?!" he exclaimed.

"Yeah," we said in unison, our enthusiasm noticeably less than his. Jan and I knew the bottle could not stay. It was inconsistent with our values, and we knew that we must somehow make it clear to Todd and our other children that graduation from high school did not exempt anyone from the standards of our home.

Jan and I talked about how to do this, pondering it for the next day or so. At the dinner table the next night, while Todd was at work, our conversation turned to his newly acquired souvenir. "Isn't Todd's beer bottle cool?" blurted Lindsay, our youngest daughter. Her reaction confirmed what I already knew; something had to be done.

During Todd's high school years, he and I had talked several times about alcohol and drinking. I had thoroughly explained my position and the biblical parameters for alcohol use. Our discussions had resulted in his decision to adopt my values as his own. He determined not to drink so that his life could have the greatest influence for God.

When Todd got home from work that night, I followed him up to his room.

"Todd," I said, in a calm voice, "I want to talk to you about your beer bottle."

His posture immediately turned defensive; he knew where this conversation was going. "Fine. Fine. I will take it out and throw it away," he said.

"No, I am not asking you to do that," I said. My response stopped him dead in his tracks. "No," I said, "I want you to defend it."

There was a moment of silence, and then he asked, "What do you mean?"

I replied, "Well, have you changed your mind about drinking and the importance of your influence on others?"

He looked at the beer bottle, then at me. "No," he said slowly.

I reminded him that in a few months he would be away at college, and in his dorm and fraternity, there would be guys who drank. I told him that if he wanted to be an influence on the people around him, he must live consistently with his values. When guys in the dorm came by his room and saw an item like the souvenir beer bottle, they would assume that he drank too. And when he talked about God, the guys in the dorm could conclude that his relationship with the Lord was simply an intellectual, religious, or moral concept rather than a vibrant, personal, interactive, love-relationship. I reminded him that our association with people, places, and things determines our influence on others, more than what we say.

A knock on the door momentarily paused our conversation. Lindsay, who was five at the time, poked her head in to remind me that she was ready for me to pray with her and tuck her into bed. Suddenly, her eyes caught the souvenir beer bottle, and her face lit up. "Hey Todd," she exclaimed, "I think your beer bottle is really cool!"

When she shut the door, I looked at Todd and said, "I rest my case. In one night, your association with this bottle has sent a message. Is it the message you want to send? Is this the kind of influence you want to have on the people around you?"

"No," he replied.

I reminded him that he could not say it wasn't cool to drink if at the same time he represented that it was cool to have a souvenir beer bottle. "The inconsistency will confuse the people around you," I told him.

I left the room to pray with Lindsay and to allow Todd some time to think about our conversation. I did not ask him to remove his souvenir because the issue was not the souvenir itself; it was the message of inconsistency the souvenir represented and the shadow it placed over his influence on others (a ready example being his siblings). That night, Todd hauled his souvenir to the trash. He realized that even if it was "really cool," it was an object inconsistent with his values.

In evaluating our children's behavior, we must realize that the issue at hand is not always the "real" issue needing to be addressed. A concerned father once came to me about the appearance of his teenage son who had recently had his ear pierced and was talking about getting a tattoo. The father wanted to know how he should deal with his son on this issue.

> *In evaluating our children's behavior, we must realize that the issue at hand is not always the "real" issue needing to be addressed.*

First, I questioned the father about his personal life and what piercings and tattoos represent to him, reminding him that it is impossible to transfer something we do not possess for ourselves. I told him that he needed to make sure that what his life represented was consistent with the value he wanted to reinforce in his son. As I talked with this father about his own life and the values he held, the discussion enabled us to discover and clarify why he was concerned about his son's appearance.

In this father's understanding, an earring was an outward sign of rebellion or defiance. He did not want his son identified by such a stereotype even if it was stylish within his age group. Once we identified the underlying value that formed the basis for his concern, it gave the father a platform to discuss it with his son. As it turns out, when he approached his son to discuss the issue, the father agreed to allow him to keep a modest earring, acknowledging that it might not have to indicate rebellion or defiance. His son listened to the father's concern about what his appearance might indicate to others and decided not to get a tattoo.

Of course, your issues may be different than the ones I am describing. They are different with each child, and they may even be more serious than the ones presented here. No matter what the issues are, I can assure you that the principles for influencing your children toward godliness will work. Uncover the value represented by your concern, check to make sure your own actions are consistent with the values you are seeking to transfer or reinforce in your child, and present your concern in a loving and relational way.

Make It Fun to Focus on God

I am completely convinced that God is into fun. The Bible tells us that He takes great pleasure in our joy and celebration before Him:

The Lord your God in your midst,

The Mighty One, will save;

He will rejoice over you with gladness ...

He will rejoice over you with singing (Zephaniah 3:17).

Of course, we must also teach our children to have reverence for God. *Most importantly, we must present God in a positive light in everything we say and do.*

Until our children reached their teen years, I would sing and pray with them before bedtime. On many evenings, I would gather all four kids in a bedroom, and with my guitar in hand, I would lead them in singing praise to God. The kids had great fun dancing, jumping on the bed, and sometimes running down the hall. "Why not?" I thought. "We're celebrating here!" Their fun-loving excitement filled me with joy. I can only imagine how pleasing it must have been to God.

To keep them focused on God, I required them to sing as they celebrated. Jan required that we keep the merriment to a dull roar. In our home, we successfully imparted our values to our children in a positive atmosphere of fun and celebration. Today, our children are adults. All—without exception—have deeply

committed, personal relationships with Christ. All—
without exception—have accepted the values we sought
to transfer.

Jan and I do not have any special abilities that guaranteed the successful transfer of our values to our children.
Everyone can do what we have done. The only requirement is that you must live what you teach and teach it
in such a way that your children can understand and
embrace it.

A Concluding Thought

"Which is the greatest commandment in the law?" a
lawyer asked Jesus. Jesus said to him, "You shall love the
Lord your God with all your heart, with all your soul, and
with all your mind" (Matthew 22:36).

In other words, Jesus said to love God with everything that you are—love Him with your whole being.
Translating that love to our children requires a positive,
personal example. It also requires us to create and
maintain an atmosphere of consistent instruction and
positive, love-centered accountability for each member
of the family.

Through our discussion in this chapter, you may have
realized that you are lacking in your example to your
children. You may have felt convicted concerning some
inconsistency in your behavior or values, or maybe your

commitment to God has become religious or boring. God is a God of grace and will accept your response to Him.

> "Come now and let us reason together,"
> says the LORD,
> "Though your sins are like scarlet,
> They shall be as white as snow;
> Though they are red like crimson,
> They shall be as wool.
> If you are willing and obedient,
> you shall eat of the good of the land" (Isaiah 1:18–19).

Don't delay. Make the necessary changes today. Walking the walk, never wasting an opportunity, being consistent, and making it fun to focus on God will help you form an effective plan. As you do this, you will ensure that your values will transfer to your children, and as God promised in Isaiah, you and your family will *eat of the good of the land.*

4

Developing a Healthy Fear of God in Your Children

Children develop a framework for understanding
God through the relationships they have with their parents,
especially the relationship they have with their father.

For many people, the fear of God is a negative
concept. He is often thought of as a menacing
figure who scrutinizes our every deed with fervor,
eagerly waiting for us to mess up so He can stir our lives
with His spoon full of wrath. This belief is revealed in
comments such as, "I don't go to church, and I know
someday I'll pay the price for it."

The perception is if we do not do what God wants us to
do, then we better be prepared to pay the price. Although
this thinking dominates western culture, ironically it has
had little influence on shaping behavior. According to
recent Gallup polls, 89% of Americans profess to believe in
God, and 79% profess to believe in a Judgment Day before
God. However, only 39% say they attend church regularly,
and only 16% say they read the Bible on a consistent basis!

The church parallels society in almost every measurable statistic: divorce, teenage pregnancy, abortion, bankruptcy, etc. Fearing God's wrath has not had any real effect on the behavior patterns of those who claim to follow God. Why is this? Simply stated, it is because *the fear of retribution does not change a heart*. Only love can accomplish that!

Why do some children avoid developing a pattern of bad behavior, and others seem drawn to it like a magnet? I believe the primary factor in determining a child's avoidance or attraction to these activities is a loving respect for his parents and a desire to make them proud. When an attitude of love and respect toward his parents does not shadow a child's decision-making process, the control mechanism intended to guide proper behavior malfunctions, opening the door to foolish actions influenced by the pressure of friends or the whim of the moment. The results can be tragic. Pranks and even more sinister deeds, such as illegal or immoral acts, are waiting to trap our children in moments of foolish indiscretion.

During my high school years, I avoided many pitfalls by using this simple method of evaluation: If I get caught, what will my parents think? My love and respect for my parents, coupled with my desire to represent them in my behavior, were governing factors that brought cautious consideration before participating in any activity. My children have used this same method to evaluate their participation in activities. In essence, this thinking represents the kind of fear that children should have for their parents—a fear of disappointing them, a fear of not properly representing them and their values. Children should never fear rejection, nor should we use the fear of rejection to motivate their behavior. *Correction is necessary, but rejection is damaging to our children.*

> ***Children should never fear rejection,
> nor should we use the fear of rejection
> to motivate their behavior.***

While I have always loved and respected my mom, it was my dad who cast the larger shadow over my consideration. I once counseled a man named Ben who was in a business that demanded a lot of time spent away from home. He thought the best way he could influence his son was to make their home the gathering point for his son's circle of friends. To ensure their home was a gathering place for the teenagers, he raised no standard for their behavior. He worried it would seem judgmental if he monitored their activities around his house. It might even drive them away! Well, Ben's plan worked. His home became a gathering place for the teenagers.

However, without a communicated and enforced standard for acceptable behavior, his home attracted the rebellious and troubled teenagers of his son's school. The negative influence of his peers began to affect the behavior of his son, so he came to me and asked what he should do. I encouraged him to set a standard for behavior consistent with the values he modeled in his own life. He needed to be kind and gracious in his enforcement of the standard but also make unwelcome any guest who was unwilling to abide by this standard. Ben could not do what I suggested because he thought it sounded too judgmental and would drive away the teenagers along with his son. He grieved when his son rebelled against him and the values he and his wife held. But he never did realize that his son's behavior was the result of his failure to be the doorkeeper of his home.

Defining the Fear of God

We cannot fully understand the fear of God and its shaping influence on behavior apart from this kind of relationship with our fathers. In its essence, the fear of God is demonstrated through attitudes and actions of reverent respect.

My father influenced our family by his character and guidance, not by intimidation. I wanted to please him because I loved and respected him. My desire to please him created a fear of disappointing him. My respect for my father and the corresponding desire to please him were never the results of fearing rejection.

Children develop a framework for understanding God through the relationships they have with their parents, especially the relationship with their father. If he is dominating, harsh, and controlling, then in the child's mind, God is also dominating, harsh, and controlling.

I have known Dave for over twenty years. He is a good father with a successful career and has been consistent in his love and service to God. However, he has always struggled to believe God really loves him, and he finds it almost impossible to imagine he could do anything that would please God. I have prayed with him many times and shared passages of Scripture to assure him that God loves him. I have shown him that the Bible is very clear that God accepts us just as we are and actually rejoices over us with singing (Zephaniah 3:17). Although this input brings momentary comfort, it doesn't stay with Dave for long. When Dave was growing up, his dad was harsh and punitive in the way he related to his son. As long as Dave pleased his dad, his dad was kind and accepting; however, if Dave ever messed up, he experienced his dad's wrath and rejection.

Although Dave is doing better today, it has been years of struggle to separate his image of God's love and acceptance from the pattern of love, acceptance, and rejection modeled by his father.

As I discussed in Chapter 2, a child's perception of God is so influenced by his relationship with his father that it is not easily changed, even with biblical references that reveal the true nature of God's love.

When understood, this truth has a profound effect on the way a father relates to his children. His actions and reactions build the children's framework for understanding God, especially in the children's primary years. The father is the image of "God" that his young children see and to which his older children relate.

Understanding the Fear of God

The foundation for a correct understanding of the fear of God is the personal confidence we have of God's approving love and affection. Most people, however, do not associate the fear of God with these terms. When correctly understood and applied, the fear of God translates into a reverent respect motivated by heartfelt love. It produces a desire to please God through attitudes and actions. When behavior has missed the mark, it is the loving respect we have for God that serves as the catalyst to produce heartfelt remorse. How is this type of response to God learned if not from the relational interaction between a father and his children?

An incident from my high school years provides an example. On a Friday night, my friends and I drove into the parking lot of an arch rival school across town to attend a basketball game. Anticipating victory, we stepped out of the car with youthful arrogance and walked toward the gym. From across the parking lot, someone yelled obscenities at us. We spun on our heels, our adrenaline pumping. In seconds, we were in a fight—with me at the center.

A police officer arrived immediately, stopped the brawl, and escorted my opponent and me (the main fighters) to the gym. I had never been a troublemaker before, so I think it surprised my high school principal to see me coming into the gym under police escort. The officer related all the details of the incident, and then my principal suspended me on the spot, pending a conversation with my father. He immediately sent me home from the game. My night was ruined.

My mom was surprised to see me arrive home early. After I told her what happened, she said, "You'll need to tell your dad when he gets home."

Dad was at a business meeting and not expected home until midnight. I suggested that since I was really tired, and she was going to be up anyway, my mom could tell him for me. She said no.

It was the longest wait of my life.

Although I was confident of his love, my heart sank as I thought of my dad's disappointment. I had let him down. I knew that my actions did not represent him or his values. It was not his punishment or retribution that I feared. It was the anticipation of his disappointment for failing to represent his values in my conduct that weighed so heavily on my thoughts.

To this day, I vividly remember my feelings that night: the cockiness on the way to the game, the machismo and adrenaline rush of the fight, and finally, the anxious anticipation of my dad's response.

When he came home, I told my dad everything, finishing with the suspension that would continue until he talked to the principal. I had disappointed myself by my actions, and I knew I had disappointed him. Without excusing my behavior, my dad affirmed his love for me and communicated his expectation that this type of behavior would not happen again. I assured him it would not. I was regretful, and he knew it.

On Monday, I waited in the secretary's office as my dad talked with the principal. After what seemed like an eternity, my dad and the principal emerged with smiles and handshakes. I returned to class, never to repeat that kind of thing again.

Respect for my dad continues to influence my life to this day. It is the essence of the "fear" I had of him, and it has formed the foundation for my "fear" of God. My dad's standards, which he established, modeled, and enforced in our home, continue to produce profound personal benefits for me. His actions built a bridge of understanding that has enabled me to receive God's loving acceptance even when I fail. His influence showed me the importance of my behavior and how it reflects, either positively or negatively, on God.

Jeff was a young man who lived in our neighborhood. His parents were good neighbors, good parents, and Jeff's dad was a leader in their church. However, Jeff's dad was busy with work and social responsibilities, and he expected his son not to cause him problems.

When Jeff was in elementary school, he had some discipline issues, and his dad was very upset with both the school and Jeff. Unfortunately, he was more concerned with the inconvenience this caused him than with the pattern it indicated in Jeff's behavior. He yelled at his son, verbally belittling him all the way from the car to the house. Jeff's dad also made sure all the neighbors knew how upset he was. However, there was no real attention to his son's behavior problem at school—just the clear message that if Jeff wanted to avoid his wrath, he'd better not inconvenience his father.

As Jeff grew into his teenage years, he became adept at slick explanations for his increasingly bizarre behavior so that his dad was appeased and not inconvenienced. The school officials and neighbors were aware of the escalating behavior problems, but because he didn't have to get involved, his dad thought Jeff was okay.

When Jeff's behavior resulted in problems with the local police and a mean, vindictive reputation among friends and neighbors, it was no longer just an issue of inconvenience. His problems now affected his dad's reputation too, both at work and in the community.

Jeff's behavior was not governed by loving respect for his parents or a desire to represent them in his actions. Jeff's dad did nothing to change this; his passive response served as a silent approval of his son's behavior. In choosing to remain passive, Jeff's dad sabotaged the mechanism God intended to help govern and guide his son; therefore, Jeff made no connection between his behavior, the reputation it produced, and the negative reflection it cast on his mom and dad.

The Connection Between Fearing Our Fathers and Fearing God

A father's primary responsibility is to establish, model, and enforce a standard for behavior in his family. While fulfilling this responsibility, he must also hold his children accountable for their behavior by giving them a pattern to follow and graciously correcting them when their behavior doesn't conform to the pattern. A desire to honor and please will not be formed in a child without this important work guided by his father. When the desire to honor and please is successfully developed, it can easily be transferred into the child's relationship with God. When there is not an attitude of respectful honor in a child for his father (and mother), a reverent respect for God will not develop either.

> *When there is not an attitude of respectful honor in a child for his father (and mother), a reverent respect for God will not develop either.*

The Bible instructs children to honor their parents and gives a command with a promise:

> Children, obey your parents in the Lord, for this is right.... "that it may be well with you and you may live long on the earth" (Ephesians 6:1,3).

A child's decision to honor his parents is developed by a father who raises and then enforces a standard through positive interactions and corrections of his children.

Some fathers confuse dependence with honor. They mistake their children's respectful requests for money, clothes, or other wants for an attitude of honor. In reality, their children's responses, though polite, may be manipulative and motivated by selfish desires.

The honor we are looking to produce in our children flows from a heart of love, not a manipulative desire to get a benefit or avoid a punishment. *Honor cannot be expressed in words only—it must be reflected in behavior.*

Many Christians today struggle with erratic patterns of behavior, never really finding the inner-discipline to live and act correctly. Rick was a single young man in our church. He struggled with a sexual sin that constantly tempted him to do what he knew was wrong. When he succumbed to the temptation, Rick was remorseful and came quickly to confess his wrong behavior—often with great sorrow. The confession, coupled with his demonstration of remorse, eased his conscience, which is a good fruit produced by repentance.

Rick's knowledge of God and the Bible produced the right words and many tears but no real or lasting effect on his actions. As we discussed his pattern of behavior, I discovered that he had no relationship with his dad. His parents were divorced, and his dad left when Rick was a young boy. Rick had no honor or respect for his father or his father's values. He had no fear represented in reverent respect for his father because his father had never been a part of his life. As a result, Rick had no fear of God.

Rick's remorse for wrong behavior was not strong enough to prevent actions that he knew were not right.

He lacked the mechanism for guiding his behavior, and he had no concept of pleasing or honoring his father, or God, through the conduct of his life.

The fear of God, represented by the desire to honor and please Him, is created through the relationship between a father and his children. *Words alone do not demonstrate the presence of reverent respect.* They must be combined with behavior consistent with the values imparted from the father. Until this relational dynamic exists between a father and his children, God's mechanism to motivate appropriate behavior will not operate properly in children's lives. God's corrective action is to ensure that our words and behavior remain consistent with His values:

> Furthermore, we have had human fathers who corrected us ... For they indeed for a few days chastened us as seemed best to them, but He for our profit, that we may be partakers of His holiness (Hebrews 12:9–10).

The purpose of God's correction is to protect us from the damage of sin so that we might enjoy the long-term benefits of His Holy Spirit in our lives—benefits such as love, joy, peace, longsuffering, kindness, and more (Galatians 5:22–23). Just believing and speaking God's standard does not produce behavior that represents Him. God disciplines, corrects, and influences His children, consistently revealing His character by never violating the individual's freedom of choice and never bringing correction through threats or intimidation.

Jesus did not force His disciples to follow Him. They followed Him by choice because they understood His character and embraced His standard of values as their own.

> From that time many of His disciples went back and walked with Him no more. Then Jesus said to the twelve, "Do you also want to go away?" But Simon Peter answered Him, "Lord, to whom shall we go? You have the words of eternal life. Also we have come to believe and know that You are the Christ, the Son of the living God" (John 6:66–69).

Simon Peter recognized that Jesus knew the right way, and he chose to follow Him! He stayed with Jesus because he came to love and respect Him, and he knew there was no one like Him. Peter was not motivated to follow God by fearing that some catastrophe would befall him if he went his own way! He responded with love to Jesus because of the character and the standard of living he saw in Him. A relationship that threatens punitive action or rejection for wrong behavior does not create the proper motivation for behavior in our children or in us.

Introducing God to our children as a Person who reacts with punitive force is the wrong method for correcting behavior. It reflects a distorted image of God and produces behavior based on a religious system of legalism and performance. Telling our children God is mad at them for certain behaviors and warning them of His impending judgment are not effective ways of changing or controlling their behavior. Instead, they are misrepresentations of God's disposition toward us.

To be sure, those who reject God should fear the punishment reserved for the final judgment. We need to inform our children of this truth. However, they must know that "Judgment Day" fear is reserved for the lost, who will experience overwhelming regret for ignoring God's loving offer of forgiveness. It will be compounded by a remorseful agreement with His judgment of their sins and the dawning horror of eternal separation from Him.

God desires a relationship of reverent respect, reflected in the attitudes and actions of His children and generated from hearts that love and sincerely seek to please Him. How do we produce this in our children? We begin by transferring our values through a clearly defined standard of behavior.

Define and Communicate Your Standard

God defined and communicated His values for humanity in the Ten Commandments. However, His love for us is not dependent upon our successful fulfillment of His laws, a truth for which we should be exceedingly grateful. Rather, His laws serve to provide us a model, a standard for behavior that properly reflects His character while revealing our need for Him.

Fathers fail to define a standard for one primary reason: we are selfish. We do not want to be accountable for our behavior. Common excuses go something like this: "I must remain open-minded." "Standards stifle creativity." In reality, these excuses only mask a rebellious unwillingness to be accountable.

Failure to define a standard leaves us with nothing to communicate and enforce within our families. Without a standard, a mishmash of rules is created and enforced only as circumstances require or if convenient in the moment. This inconsistency produces the equivalent of a moving target of values for our children. Both frustrating and confusing, it produces poor results—in target practice and in child development. If there is no standard, our efforts to train and shape our children will fail.

If there is no standard, our efforts to train and shape our children will fail.

Jim and Sue came to my office to discuss Sue's frustration with Jim and the problem it was producing in their children. It seemed that Jim was a happy, go-lucky guy—the life of any party. Sue enjoyed and appreciated this about him, but along with his easy-going, fun-loving nature came a resistance to define anything by absolutes.

As I questioned him, I found that he could not absolutely say it was wrong to steal, or to murder, or to cheat. To him, the situation determined what was appropriate. Only when I would describe the situation could he tell me if a particular action was wrong. Without knowing the situation, he was unwilling to label most any behavior as "wrong." This was the source of conflict and concern for Sue.

They could have no rules for their children because each situation determined what was right or wrong. It might or might not be wrong for one of the children to come in past curfew. Jim did not want to set a general curfew; he wanted to set it based on each event. But it went further than defining a general time the children needed to be home at night. It covered almost every area of their life.

Was it wrong to disobey the school administration? Was it wrong to break the law? To Jim, it all depended on the circumstances. I asked Jim if he had values that governed his life. He was firmly convinced that he did, but as we talked, he admitted he could not define his values apart from specific situations. Jim could not impart values to his children for behavior and living until after a situation developed, and because details changed from situation to situation, what was wrong in one situation might be fine in another.

Sue dealt firsthand with the confusion and frustration their children experienced with this moving target. How could they know what was acceptable and what was not acceptable if the standard changed with each situation? Sue recognized that without a consistent standard, any efforts to train their children and transfer their values to them would fail.

Associating Performance with Acceptance

It is just as dangerous to our children's welfare to associate love and acceptance with their performance as it is to fail to define a standard. When the motive for good behavior is the fear of rejection, our children develop a performance concept of love rather than an acceptance concept of love. They learn that they will be accepted and loved if they do right, but if they do wrong, they will be rejected. Parents teach this concept of performance acceptance when they extend love and relationship based on their children's behavior conform-ing to the expectations of their standard.

When parents establish and transfer a standard for behavior, they are defining boundaries represented by values for their children. The boundaries provide security and protection, and they are good, necessary, and beneficial for their children's development. However, a standard becomes a weapon of emotional and spiritual destruction when associated with love and acceptance. Acceptance must remain based on the relationship—never on performance.

I remind you that God does not love us based on performance. God's love is without condition. He loves us even though He knows the worst about us. *His blessings are conditional based upon our response, but His love is unconditional.*

It may seem paradoxical to love and accept our children in spite of their foolish actions. You might wonder how acceptance creates the reverent respect and the desire to please that is necessary to shape behavior. Acceptance is the reflection of love that is patient and kind, that believes all things, hopes all things, and endures all things (1 Corinthians 13). Rejection does not create acceptance of our values, honor and respect, or a desire to please. These qualities are only created through proactive love. We do not have to perform to receive God's love, and our children should not have to perform to receive our love.

If we are going to represent God to our children and transfer to them a proper understanding of His love and care, our actions must be consistent with His nature. We must teach values and uphold a standard without attaching our acceptance to successful performance. God holds us to a standard by correcting us when we miss the mark, and we must correct our children when they miss the mark. However, correction should never involve rejection.

God has separated His love and acceptance of us from the standard He has established for our behavior; we must do the same for our children. God imparts His values into our lives, and through His grace, He loves us just as we are—imperfections and all. He loves us enough to correct us when we fail to meet His standard, without rejecting us for failed efforts! This is true love, and this is the concept we want to represent and transfer to our children.

When we enforce our standard through rigid demands on our children or associate acceptance with their adherence to our standard, we create an atmosphere for legalism. Legalism is the inflexible enforcement of a standard of rules tied to performance.

Jimmy Swaggart's much-publicized fall from ministry in the late 1980s and early 1990s provides an example of this truth. Swaggart is a gifted musician, songwriter, and preacher. He was the founder and leader of a dynamic, worldwide ministry. Leading up to his public embarrassment and removal from ministry (he was caught in a motel room with a prostitute), he could be seen preaching an unbending standard of holy and righteous living.

Jimmy Swaggart passionately preached against immorality, adultery, and pornography. His rigid application of biblical passages raised a standard for right living, but it also created an atmosphere for legalism and self-righteousness. Ultimately, the legalism that enforced the standard he raised became a covering for his own unrighteous behavior—behavior that was contrary and inconsistent with the message he preached. His presentation of the standard was inflexible and offered no grace for failure.

Our parenting goal is not to create a standard of behavior that becomes a tool of destruction to our children. Paul and Sally are a couple who love God and serve Him with passion. They live a life of commitment to God and demonstrate a high standard of behavior based on the values they live and believe. However, their four children are a mess, each having rejected the values of their parents as they matured into their upper teens and early twenties. They refused to adopt their parents' standard as their own.

Why? How does a committed couple, passionate in their love and service for God, fail to pass their values on to their children? The answer lies in the application and enforcement of their standard. Paul and Sally left no room for their children to grow into their service and passion for God. It was expected and demanded. It was legislated.

An attitude of resistance was labeled as rebellion. If their children's passions turned toward sports, dating, cars, clothes, or other teenage interests, their parents questioned their love for God. They left no room for failure to achieve their standard, even with diligent effort on their children's behalf. Over time, this rigid application produced angry rejection in all their children for Paul and Sally's standard. It brought disappointment and heartbreak to the parents, along with a crushing sense of failure.

Paul and Sally's high standard and expectations of proper behavior did not produce the response they desired in their children. Legalism perverts the proper fear of God, replacing it with a cheap substitute, not based on love and honor, but on performance and rules. Legalism is a harsh taskmaster that, without exception, produces rejection of the standard and rebellion to the values.

Avoid the Two Extremes of Legalism

Legalism is acceptance with strings attached.

When legalism is present, it is commonly found in one of two dangerous extremes. The first extreme is to raise the standard but have no method of enforcement. The father may have communicated his standards to his children, yet he allows his children to live below the standard because he feels no one can completely live up to the standard he has raised. In this situation, mercy overrules truth. The relationship is valued, but the standard for measuring behavior is compromised. There is no accountability.

At the beginning of this chapter, I told the story of Ben and his reaction to raising and enforcing a standard in his home. He placed such a high value on the relationship with his son that he compromised his values, to the detriment of everyone in the home.

The second extreme is to connect the standard to the relationship—if you don't measure up, you lose the relationship. Paul and Sally's children were always in trouble for failing to live up to their parents' standard. These harsh and punitive punishments isolated the children from the family as the parents attempted to drive home their disappointment with pain and rejection.

In this extreme, truth overrules mercy. Value is placed solely on performance, and the quality of the relationship is compromised. When love and respect do not motivate our children to adopt our standard of behavior, something is wrong. Forcing the correct behavior through threats of rejection might work for a short while, but it will not sustain a permanent lifestyle of proper behavior. It will ultimately produce resentment and destroy the relationship between parents and their children. Only loving acceptance in addition to a clearly defined standard will create the desire in our children to make us proud of their behavior.

Only loving acceptance in addition to a clearly defined standard will create the desire in our children to make us proud of their behavior.

A Concluding Thought

If you grew up with an abusive or domineering father, this chapter may have reminded you of painful memories. Based on your experiences, it may be difficult for you to comprehend the idea of loving respect for your father as a motive for proper behavior and to embrace it as the basis for loving and respecting for God. It may be hard to see God in any other light than that of your father's treatment of you. You may even struggle with abusive or dominant tendencies toward your own children.

Even if your experience has not been positive, it is important to understand this concept in relation to developing a healthy relationship with God and living a life pleasing to Him. Do you respect and honor your father? Do your children honor and respect you? Do they have a loving desire to please you? Or do you relate to them through the fear of intimidation or abusive dominance? Do you accept or reject them based on their performance?

If you need to forgive your father for his failure, whether through neglect or abuse, why not take a moment to offer up a prayer of forgiveness? Ask God to help you forgive your father and heal the hurts of your childhood. Ask Him to help you understand for yourself how to raise a standard for behavior without linking acceptance to performance. Ask God to help you train your children to honor and respect you in a healthy way so that they will live their adult lives with honor and respect for Him. God will answer your prayer and teach you His ways.

Section Two

Transferring Standards

5

A Matter of Character

God's work performed in God's way produces God's results.
He is not impressed by results that have been produced
using methods inconsistent with His nature.

During presidential elections in the United States, the subject of character is a topic of heated debate. Many insist character flaws are irrelevant as long as the presidential candidate can do the job well. Once in office, presidents are often measured by the results they produce, rather than by the character standards they uphold. When results are the only measuring stick for success, character becomes excluded, and a door is opened for dangerous, immoral, or unethical behavior to be accepted. The Bible tells us, "Righteousness exalts a nation, but sin is a reproach to any people" (Proverbs 14:34).

Character does not mean perfection. It does not establish authority for self-righteousness and intolerance. Instead, character relates to our standards and values. It forms the framework for the expression of our personalities and talents. It is the moral and ethical structure for our actions—the bedrock of our thinking and the basis for our treatment of others and our response to circumstances. If left unchallenged or uncorrected, character flaws become strongholds of weakness that control an individual and cause pain to those closest to him.

> *If left unchallenged or uncorrected, character flaws become strongholds of weakness that control an individual and cause pain to those closest to him.*

Almost everyone has exaggerated circumstances when retelling a story to a friend or family members. However, when exaggeration becomes a pattern of communication, it must be addressed. *Exaggerations are lies in seed form.* The step from an exaggeration to a deliberate manipulation of truth (a lie) is not a very big step. A pattern of lying reveals the character flaw of dishonesty.

Therefore, we must treat even small issues with serious-minded resolve. We cannot allow bad attitudes to be tolerated or go unchallenged because attitudes generate thoughts, thoughts lead to actions, actions develop habits, habits form character, and character determines destiny!

Imagine beginning a long trip in a car with a flawed tire. This flawed tire may perform adequately on short drives around town and may even go unnoticed for a number of miles at high speed. Yet the potential for disaster is always present. A blowout on the highway could result in severe injuries, even death. Those who have experienced this understand firsthand the seriousness of a minor flaw left unchecked.

Imagine being in business with a person who is dishonest. Perhaps his character flaw shows up in pressure situations when he is threatened with loss, hurt, or rejection. In the face of this kind of pressure, he will do anything to avoid personal pain. Let's presume that in the natural growth of your business, a crisis inevitably develops, possibly one like this: your business becomes strapped for capital, and it looks like you and your partner need to take less income from the business in order to survive the crisis. Your partner is responsible for the accounting operations, and to avoid the personal sacrifice associated with the cutback, he begins embezzling funds from the business. His character flaw has now affected the day-to-day conduct of your business. Under routine circumstances it didn't show up, but under the pressure of this crisis, it has been revealed. The potential devastation to you and your business is incalculable, even to the point of threatening its very existence.

Character determines our responses to difficult situations in our lives. When we speak of character, we speak
of qualities such as faithfulness, honesty, diligence,
loyalty, bravery, generosity, patience, and the ability to
receive correction. Even a cursory look at this list should
make the significance of character apparent.

Who wants to enter into any important endeavor with
someone of questionable character? Would you want to
put your life on the line and depend on someone who
lacked character qualities? Every day we rely upon the
character of people. We trust in the president of the
United States as our commander in chief to lead the
military in defending our nation. We call upon police
and law enforcement personnel to enforce the law and
make our communities safe. And we depend upon count-
er-terrorism units to thwart disasters, such as the one
that brought down the Twin Towers of the World Trade
Center on September 11, 2001.

Almost everywhere we look, we depend upon the
character of the people around us to perform their jobs.
We rely on character so much that it is often taken for
granted until someone without character makes a choice
that confronts us with destructive results.

Over many years of conducting premarital counseling, I have found one of the most important aspects of
marriage preparation is to identify and correct character
flaws. When I meet with a couple, I ask them for details

about their individual lives, apart from the life they are developing together. I ask them about their work experience and how many jobs they have held. Through the answers to these questions, I look for signs that indicate a character weakness like laziness or slothful attitudes or behavior.

Craig and Rachel were a young engaged couple I was counseling in preparation for their wedding day. As we talked, Craig revealed he had been at his current job almost a year. He commented to Rachel that this was the longest time he had ever been at one job in his life. Craig was in his mid-twenties, and his comment raised a red flag in my mind. Faithfulness, diligence, and the willingness to work hard are qualities that reflect character. They are also qualities critical to the long-term success of a marriage.

Early in my pastoral ministry, I would have overlooked a comment like Craig's, failing to realize the connection. But after a few couples whose wedding ceremonies I conducted went on to divorce, I began to make a connection. I realized that character issues impact all areas of life.

As I worked with Craig in counseling, I found he did have a character weakness that affected his employment. We worked to correct and identify attitudes of laziness and behaviors that made him unreliable as an employee. Craig worked hard to change his behavior and thinking, which not only helped him to become a better employee but also prepared him to succeed in marriage.

I can't think of any couple I have encountered through my pastoral ministry that expected one of the partners to be unfaithful or fail to fulfill their responsibilities in the marriage. Despite our best efforts, though, we all fall short of perfection. Some people fail at critical points of character weakness, whether in marriage, friendship, or on the job. Critical failure based on a character flaw is devastating. So, you ask if character really is that important? Absolutely!

Regardless of talent, we cannot develop into the people God desires or fulfill His destiny for our lives apart from our character. It is true that individuals who lack character can accomplish noteworthy deeds if these deeds are measured only by results like the power of their influence, their net worth, or even their physical size. Eventually, though, deficiency in character exacts its price—whether in family relations, personal health, reputation, finances, or some other area.

To become president of the United States is a noteworthy accomplishment. Several presidents, however, have faced questions of character, not only while in the Oval Office but throughout their political careers. Any achievement produced without character is temporary; any effort solely focused on results will not satisfy, especially when measured by God in the light of eternity.

Any achievement produced without
character is temporary.

To accomplish truly great things with lasting results,
our efforts must align with God's plans and His methods.
God's work performed in God's way produces God's results.
He is not impressed by results that have been produced
using methods inconsistent with His nature.

Mankind's character was intended to be a direct
reflection of the nature of God. He is the essence of
true character; everything good, wholesome, and pure
begins in Him. It does not matter what our motives
are, or if the results are for a good cause. When we
lie, cheat, or steal to get the desired result, God is not
impressed. In His system, the end never justifies the
means.

Just as parents know their children's behavior is a
reflection on them, God also knows that if we claim
to be His followers, our behavior is a reflection on
Him. Therefore, He expects us to live our lives in ways
that represent and reflect His character. Through the
partnership established between God and parents,
character is emphasized and developed in children. In
his role as the leader of the family, it becomes a father's
responsibility to represent and reinforce the qualities of
God's character in his children.

How Is Character Developed?

In the New Testament, James gives us an understanding of God's method of character development. The pattern is laid out in the first chapter:

> My brethren, count it all joy when you fall into various trials, knowing that the testing of your faith produces patience. But let patience have its perfect work, that you may be perfect and complete, lacking nothing (James 1:2–4).

The trials associated with difficult circumstances produce qualities that cannot be developed in any other way. As we walk through challenging circumstances with our eyes of faith focused on God, a good thing happens. Like the muscles of a weightlifter after a strenuous workout, our character is strengthened through adversity. Tough circumstances may leave us emotionally and spiritually exhausted, but the process works to produce greater strength of character.

James describes this process of shaping us into the likeness of God as a necessary work to make us complete. Each trial or circumstance molds necessary qualities into our lives for completeness, so nothing necessary to fulfill God's plan will be lacking. A father who embraces this process in his own life is equipped to recognize and support its work in his children's lives as well.

Character is developed and strengthened through an often-painful process, one each of us would like to avoid, whether as children or adults. However, when the process has worked its way to completion, it develops God's nature in us.

Character development is a step-by-step process. It takes time. Like a chef creating a culinary masterpiece, ingredients are added in measured amounts—not all at once but at just the right time in the cooking process to produce a dish that delights the taste buds and satisfies the appetite. Character is created through a similar process. God measures out situations based on our level of maturity, adding complications at just the right moment to test our values, expose our weak areas, and ultimately round out our character. The process produces a masterpiece of individual character, stronger and more complete than ever before.

We refer to a person who has been shaped by this process as one who has *integrity*, which means "incorruptibility and completeness." A person of integrity is a person with well-rounded character.

Situations arise daily and demand a response; some are more difficult than others. The more difficult ones test the fiber of our being, exposing weaknesses and imperfections. This is how character develops. Shielding our children from trials and difficult circumstances subverts the process of making them well-rounded individuals armed with the character of God. Parents who are unaware of this process are under the misconception that by defending their children, they are protecting them. In actuality, they are undermining character development.

> *Shielding our children from trials*
> *and difficult circumstances subverts*
> *the process of making them*
> *well-rounded individuals armed*
> *with the character of God.*

Parents play a beneficial role when they work with their children to discover the lessons to be learned in difficult situations, rather than being their child's defender against all perceived injustice. When there is physical danger or emotional abuse, it is our responsibility as parents to step into the situation to protect our children. Otherwise, if things are simply not going their way, we need to work with our children to identify and embrace the situation as a developmental test from God. If we skirt around the test, it just means they will have to take it again under different circumstances.

Trinity Fellowship Church had a kindergarten through twelfth grade accredited school. During a period in the school's history when the students were required to wear uniforms, the policy stated that a uniform sweater was to be worn before a jacket could be added in the classroom during cold or inclement weather.

During one winter season, a student wore a jacket to class. The teacher reminded the student that the policy required her to wear a uniform sweater before wearing a jacket and asked her to remove the jacket while in class. The student objected, telling the teacher she didn't own a uniform sweater because her parents thought it was unnecessary. She refused to remove her jacket, stating she was too cold. The teacher then sent her to the principal's office where the policy was enforced, and the student was made to remove her jacket before being allowed to return to class.

When the student informed her parents of the situation, they were furious with the teacher and the school administration. They did not agree with the uniform policy and its enforcement by the teacher. The parents felt the teacher was heartless because she did not allow their daughter to be warm in class, even if the jacket did violate the uniform policy.

The parents stepped in to right the injustice of this situation. They mounted a campaign to get the teacher removed and the policy overturned. They sought to organize a parent boycott if the school did not meet their demands.

As you read this account, you may side with the parents in believing the teacher was too rules-centered and insensitive to the physical needs of a student in her class. You may also think the parents were right in coming to the defense of their child. This type of response is becoming more common in situations involving perceived injustices from authorities in children's lives.

However, it is this type of response that undermines character development in our children.

As adults, we know life is not always fair. Most of us have experienced some form of injustice from authorities. But in this student's case, there was no compelling reason for the parents to step in—no physical danger represented by the teacher's response, no emotional scarring from their daughter being cold in class. Discomfort? Yes. Compelling danger? No.

What were the character issues involved in this situation? What should the parents have done to support the development of their child's character? The issues in development were submission to authority and faith in God's ability to bring justice to any situation. To support these important lessons, the parents should have comforted their daughter, giving her the compassion she missed from the teacher and principal. Then they should have told her they would immediately purchase a uniform sweater. They should have admitted their mistake in not purchasing the sweater along with the other uniform pieces. In short, the parents should have supported the rules of the teacher and school administration, thereby teaching their daughter the importance of respecting authority. Finally, for their own strength of resolve in the situation, the parents should have maintained the perspective that God can change any situation they don't like while protecting their daughter. He is able to right all injustice. The key is to respond with the right attitude.

Lessons Form Character

At the age of thirteen, I learned an important lesson in character development, one which my dad could have easily undermined had he not reacted in the proper way.

It was summer, and I decided to mow lawns for extra money. With my parents' approval, I canvassed the neighborhood and soon found my first customer: a nice widow who lived behind the church parking lot next to our house. She was very particular in the way she kept her lawn. She expected the grass clippings to be carried to the trash, and she wanted the driveway and walks to be edged neatly. I quoted her my price, and the next day she called to find out how soon I could start.

"I have out-of-town guests coming to visit," she said, "and I want the lawn to look good for their arrival." We agreed on a date for me to begin servicing her lawn.

When the day arrived, I was not in the mood. A neighborhood baseball game at the elementary school by our house caught my interest, and I promptly forgot about my commitment to my customer, the condition of her lawn, and her out-of-town guests who were to arrive later that day.

As my family sat down to dinner that evening, the widow's lawn was a distant memory in my mind. Then the telephone rang. It was my customer, demanding to know why I had not mowed her lawn. She was upset and disappointed.

Unfortunately, my dad had answered the call. When he discovered I had failed to keep my word, he apologized to her and said I would be right over. I tried to convince my dad that I should cut my loss in this situation. "After all," I said, "I've messed up, and she's mad at me. Why should I go and confront her in her anger? Why not let her get someone else to mow her lawn? I can start fresh with a new customer another day."

My response so irritated my dad that he accompanied me over to the widow's house and stood there while I apologized. As I mowed, hauled the grass to the trash, and edged the walks, he and the widow critiqued my work while enjoying a neighborly conversation. When I finished, my dad made sure that I apologized again, and then he did something completely unexpected—he refused to let her pay me for the work!

To make matters worse, the widow told me that because I had not kept my word, she could not trust me and therefore would not keep me as her lawn boy. She concluded by telling me again how disappointed she was in me. This humiliating situation etched into my character a lesson of faithfulness that I have never forgotten.

I have observed many parents who react the exact opposite of the way my dad did. It is as if they condone and encourage character flaws. With co-dependent unhealthiness, they defend the incorrect behavior of their children, attacking anyone who points out flaws and making that person the issue, rather than requiring their children to correct their behavior. Sadly, when an opportunity is missed, not only is it gone, but it's actually done harm to the child's character. Therefore, parents must be on watch and make the most of every opportunity to mold character.

> *Parents must be on watch and*
> *make the most of every opportunity*
> *to mold character.*

A Lifelong Work

My dad's example benefited Jan and me many times over the years in rearing our family. Learning lessons of character helped me recognize opportunities to teach character to each of our children. Lessons of character continue to present themselves through a variety of situations that impact Jan and me individually, us as a couple, and each of our children. *Character development is a lifelong work.*

Each of our children has played some level of competitive sports. Athletics offer ample trials that test, mold, and perfect character. These trials include the amount of playing time, the coach's treatment of players, personal discipline, diligent preparation, maintaining the right attitude in competition, etc.

At a relatively young age, our oldest son, Todd, demonstrated above-average athletic ability. When he was five years old, I started working with him to develop his basketball skills. Todd was better than most of his peers, and he loved the game. When the morning of tryouts for the "Little Dribblers" basketball team finally arrived, Todd was determined to make the team. Jan and I thought he was a cinch to be drafted because of his skill and the relationships we had with several of the coaches.

When the tryouts were finished and team selections were posted, Todd was not chosen. Disappointed and feeling the stun of rejection, he convinced himself that he had not been selected due to his lack of ability. His self-esteem plunged as he declared himself a terrible player. In addition, Jan and I were hurt and confused; we could not understand why our son had not been selected. It was tempting to be angry and bitter, lashing out at the people involved in the selection process; however, we knew this response was not right, nor would it help our son deal with his disappointment.

We were scrambling to make "lemonade" from the "lemons" of this situation when a league official announced that a second league would be formed. The new league would incorporate all the boys who had not been selected to play in the original league; no one would be left out.

With some degree of coaxing on our part, Todd agreed to play in what he called the "losers' league." I told him he was a good player with good skills and would most likely enjoy extra playing time in the new league, which he might not have had if he had been selected to play on a team in the first draft. I encouraged him to work hard and do his best because I knew good things happen when we make a proper response to circumstances. Both Jan and I assured him that diligent effort, good attitude, patience, and steadfast commitment would pay off in the long run. How did we know? Because these are the qualities of character, and character always prevails!

Todd joined the new league and was an influential player. He was selected to the all-star team, and it ended as a good basketball experience. He went on to play high school basketball and was a varsity player during his junior and senior years. Upon graduation, he was selected to play on the regional all-star team. Diligence, good attitude, patience, and steadfast commitment paid off well.

If I had not understood the potential impact of situations on the development of character, the basketball story would have been a painful family memory from our son's youth. However, because of our influence, the difficult situation ended with good results and produced some great basketball memories for our family. Memories are great, but more important are the qualities of character that are developed, tested, and tempered through trials. We must not rob our children of character development by shielding them from tough situations.

At all stages and ages of our children's development, situations will arise that seem unjust, unfair, cause hurt and tears, and overwhelm them—testing their ability to respond correctly. This situation was very traumatic for Todd, though not as traumatic as breaking up with his first girlfriend, or rear-ending another car at a stoplight and totaling his car, or being detained by airport security for his comment about a concealed weapon.

You may be facing circumstances or situations that are much more severe than the issues I faced with Todd, but the truth of God's principles apply to every situation. They will give you solid direction as you walk with your children through their difficulties, developing their character and deepening their trust in God.

Tests of Character Never Stop

I once heard someone say that God's tests are pass/fail, meaning you keep taking a test until you pass it. Character development is not just for children; tests of character continue right through adulthood. In this sense, we have something in common with our children—God is still molding and developing our character even as we are working with Him to shape theirs.

In the early years of my business career, I faced a test of character on the job. I was the assistant merchandising manager for one of my company's marketing regions. My department purchased all the products for the sales force to market in the company's southwest division. One of our largest customers was the state government and its related agencies. It was my responsibility to order the products we sold to them under special pricing from our suppliers. It was also my responsibility to keep accurate records of purchases by the different agencies, quarterly reporting the sales volume associated with the state contract to our suppliers.

One morning my boss walked into my office and asked me to place an order for 80,000 pounds of printing paper for one of our customers. As he left to return to his office, he instructed me to enter the order as a state contract purchase. There was just one problem—this particular customer was not a state agency.

What was I to do? Ignore his request or enter the order and thereby join in his dishonesty? After an hour of internal struggle and debate, the nature of which tests the strength and integrity of personal character, I determined that I could not enter the order. If the order was to be entered, I resolved my boss would have to do it himself. I was prepared to stand my ground, even if it cost me my job.

Later in the day, my boss returned to my desk. I assumed he wanted to check on the status of the order, but to my surprise and before I could tell him of my resolve, he said he had changed direction with the customer and no longer needed the order. As he rushed out of my office and on to his next appointment, he told me to cancel it.

The test of my character in this situation was the process of thought that led me to the internal commit-ment to quit my job before lying to our supplier. In effect, it was a simulation. It looked real, felt real, and required a response as if it was real, but the action never fully materialized.

Sometimes circumstances create a simulation to test character. In this case, the conditions caused me to wrestle with issues in my heart that tested and revealed the qualities and strength of my character. Luckily, the process stopped short of requiring me to act on what I determined was the appropriate course of action during the test.

Airline pilots understand this type of training. They regularly have their flight skills tested and certified by being presented with very real flight situations through the use of a simulator. A simulator is a computerized apparatus that mimics flight conditions and tests a pilot's ability to react to them. With an evaluator looking on, the pilot responds to various conditions that test his responses to tough flight situations before encountering them for real.

We never know which test will include the requirement to act on what we have determined is right and which test will end up being just a simulation. *Therefore, we must treat every test as though it is real.*

Simulated or real, tests reveal character. The process of testing trains, prepares, and strengthens our character to meet the challenges of everyday life. God is our evaluator in these tests; He monitors our thoughts and our intended actions. As with the airline pilots, when we think and act correctly, it is as if God certifies us as capable of withstanding the stress on our character presented by the circumstances of life.

A Concluding Thought

Character is developed by recognizing and using the daily tests of life to train, mold, and perfect specific qualities that are missing from our children's character. We must also understand that these tests change from year to year as our children mature.

It is important to teach our children to trust God above people and to develop in them the desire to choose right over wrong in the midst of circumstances, regardless of fairness or feelings. As we do this, we partner with God in His work to test, strengthen, and perfect our children's character. As the Scripture says, "Train up a child in the way he should go, and when he is old he will not depart from it" (Proverbs 22:6).

6

Faith's Influence on Character Development

Regardless of the details, which differ in each circumstance,
faith always asks for our response. Will it be a response
of trust in God's faithfulness, or will it be a response
that takes matters into our own hands?

F aith is confident trust in the character of God. In very practical terms, it is like glasses used to correct vision. Through faith, we gain the ability to see God's work in all situations. Faith lays the foundation for trust in God. It is not driven or determined by emotions but instead is anchored in God's Word. Through faith, we gain God's perspective on situations, seeing them in a completely different light. Faith gives us the ability to be completely confident that God is working in our circumstances, even though our eyes may not see it and our logic has yet to confirm it. When faith is at work, it overrules feelings and frees us from anxiety, panic, and other thoughts that battle for control of our lives, applying pressure on us to act independently of God's will.

Faith gives us the ability to be completely confident that God is working in our circumstances, even though our eyes may not see it and our logic has yet to confirm it.

Notice as I have defined faith, it has not been in the context of church attendance or a religious institution. You and I are people of faith, not because we attend church or belong to a religious organization, but because we see the connection of three interdependent truths:

- God is present and intimately involved in the circumstances of life.
- His promises are true and have universal application.
- Our sincere efforts toward the personal application of His promises will produce results.

When actions are based on these precepts, faith acts as the rudder that steers the ship and the fuel that enables its forward motion. It moves out of the realm of religious thought into what God intended: an active agent that influences perspective and energizes behavior. *Through faith, circumstances don't rule us—we rule them.*

Parents enter into a partnership with God by faith as He uses circumstances to fashion character in their children. Circumstances are the kiln used to bake the qualities of character to their finished strength and appearance. The "firing" process produces brilliantly glazed qualities of character such as honesty, diligence, loyalty, bravery, generosity, patience, and the ability to receive correction well. When faith is added to any circumstance, it provides protection for the vessel (the child) and ensures that damage does not occur in the "firing" process. Parents who attempt to create the qualities of character on their own, without the support of faith, must depend on their own wisdom and experience—something God never intended.

Walking by Faith

Circumstances create opportunities for faith to influence our behavior. Faith also keeps us from responding to issues based on our feelings. Here is a real-life example from my family:

The year Jan and I celebrated our eighth anniversary, circumstances presented a critical need. Tyler, our third child, had made his entrance into our family, and our house had become cramped. We needed more living space to accommodate our growing family, so we began to seek God about moving.

One major obstacle stood in our path. The early 1980s was a time of double-digit inflation. Inflation was steeply driving up the purchase price of homes, and mortgage interest rates climbed right along with them. We felt God's release to begin looking for a new home for our family, but the search was very frustrating. When we found a house that would meet our needs, the 18% mortgage interest rate made the payment out of reach for our family's budget. Knowing our need, Jan's parents made a generous offer of financial help to enable us to get into a larger home.

Finally, our search turned up a "fixer upper" home comprised of everything we required: four bedrooms, an open and spacious kitchen, a large living area, and lots of storage. Although it needed to be updated, we were willing to fix it up because the condition brought the sales price into our budget's range. More importantly, the home had an assumable mortgage. In other words, it had a mortgage that could be assumed simply by paying the sellers their equity amount (the difference between the sales price and the mortgage amount of the note).

The money we needed to assume the seller's note exceeded the proceeds we were going to receive from the sale of our home, requiring a significant financial commitment from Jan's parents. Although we had not discussed the amount of their commitment, we moved forward. At the recommendation of our realtor, we decided to wait until our home sold before making a formal offer on the "fixer upper." Our realtor advised us that the sale of our home would allow us to offer a quick closing on the purchase of the other home, something she believed would be attractive to the seller and hopefully secure us the lowest possible purchase price.

We set things in motion, believing God was answering our prayers. In a few days, our home sold for the full asking price. It so happened that this was on the same weekend Jan's parents came for a visit. It seemed like perfect timing to show them our "fixer upper" and talk about the specific details of the purchase contract.

Two obstacles soon developed. First, as I previously mentioned, we had not discussed with Jan's parents the specific amount they would need to contribute to allow the purchase to take place. In the rush of activities surrounding the sale of our home and the purchase of our new one, Jan and I had assumed too much. When we finally sat down with Jan's parents to discuss the details, we found they had a different amount in mind than we did. Although we had been praying for God's leading in each decision regarding our move, the circumstances were changing, and things were not working out as we expected.

We were faced with a major question—were we going to panic under what seemed to be the shakiness of the situation? Or were we going to trust that God was working to bring about the right result? Regardless of the details, which differ in each circumstance, faith always asks for our response. Will it be a response of trust in God's faithfulness, or will it be a response that takes matters into our own hands? The decision to trust God determines if faith comes alive in our circumstance to influence the outcome, or if it remains on the sidelines, never to be activated and never to make a difference.

When Jan and I realized the miscommunication with her parents and their discomfort with the financial amount we needed, we released them from any financial obligation associated with their offer. Our answer to faith's question in this circumstance was to trust God for His provision. He would be our resource, even though we did not know how. Our response released Jan's parents from the pressure they felt to meet our need due to the quick sale of our home. Like Abraham, the father of our faith, we headed out, not knowing where we were going but trusting God was directing the circumstances and confident He would get us where we needed to go.

We had just answered faith's first question when the second obstacle presented itself. The "fixer upper" sold before we could make a formal offer on it! We had no place to go, less money than expected, and a sales contract that gave the new owners possession of our house in 30 days. We needed answers! We needed to move!

"How could this be, God?" we thought. "How could we have missed Your direction this badly?" We felt panic, but our faith overpowered our panic, reorienting our perspective. We began to see that God had something different for us. Faith once again presented a question, and our response was still to trust God and believe in His work before our eyes could see the reality of it. Our faith was grounded in the Scripture that says, "Your Father knows what you have need of before you ask Him." (Matthew 6:8)

We were confident God would lead us to a good place and teach us new things about Himself in the process. Our attention turned toward building a new home. Jan looked through plans, and I began to search for a lot. We found a rental home for the interim. The rent was almost twice the amount of our old house payment—for much less house. Nevertheless, faith influenced our actions and gave us the perspective that God was leading us to a better place.

We were moving ahead with plans for a new home when a friend told us about a large, two-story house that had been on the market for some time. She encouraged us to take a look and said we might be surprised to find it in our price range.

The house turned out to be bigger and better than the "fixer upper" we had not been able to purchase, and this one was move-in ready. Through our realtor, we negotiated a purchase price with favorable financing and moved into the house using only the equity from the sale of our former home. God's hand was at work on our behalf.

God had guided our steps, and through actions of faith, we now possessed the house He had been preparing for us all along. To make things even better, Jan's parents purchased new carpet for the entire house! The carpet was a very generous gift that enhanced the look of our new home and was more in line with their thinking when they made their offer to help. Everyone was pleased, and we lived in that house for 20 years. It was God's blessing to us!

Once again, let me say that we can only transfer to our children what we possess for ourselves. We must allow faith to determine our perspective in the circumstances of life so that through our experiences, we can be in a position to influence and support God's work in our children. Faith anchors our character to God by keeping our attention and dependence focused upon Him.

Faith anchors our character to God by keeping our attention and dependence focused upon Him.

Faith's Influence

Is God at work in every situation? This must be our understanding and perspective for faith to have its proper influence. Jesus told His disciples not to worry about the circumstances of their lives. He assured them that God knew *every* need and situation, and they could have confidence that He would care for them (Luke 12:22–34).

I know this truth. I believe it and attempt to apply it to my perspective in every circumstance. However, there are times when I need my wife or a close friend to remind me of this truth, encourage me in the situation, and bolster my faith by inserting some of their faith where mine has become weak. This is especially true when I have not seen any change in a situation after waiting for a long time.

In these moments, I need the strength and influence of someone else's faith to encourage and bolster mine. Because I am aware of this need in my life, I am sensitive to the fact that my children also have this need in their own lives. It is my God-ordained responsibility as their father to influence their perspective with my faith.

Several years ago, as I enjoyed my morning quiet time on a business trip, my thoughts centered on my oldest daughter, Lisa, who was attending the University of Nebraska in Omaha. She was dating a young man who had graduated from college and was pursuing his career.

I had concerns about the relationship. I worried they might get serious about marriage without addressing important issues in their relationship. I was concerned Lisa might compromise the qualities she really wanted in a husband just to be married.

I prayed about my concerns as I read my Bible and wrote in my journal. I felt like the Lord gave me a message for Lisa, so I recorded the impression in my journal. Later that day I called Lisa, as I regularly did, and her dating situation came up in our conversation. I took the opportunity to tell her about the message the Lord gave me that morning. It went something like this: God wanted Lisa to know that if she would not compromise her standard for a husband, He would bring a husband to her at the right time. I told her this word was a promise for her, to be remembered as she dated and considered marriage. The promise was God would bring her the husband of her dreams, a man prepared by God to meet her needs, if she would patiently wait for Him to finish His work. This special man would not require her to compromise her standards or lessen her desires related to a husband. God was preparing him to meet her needs and fulfill all her dreams. Jeremiah 29:11 says:

> "For I know the thoughts that I think toward you, says the LORD,
> thoughts of peace and not of evil, to give you a future and a hope."

Confident that this message represented God, I delivered it to Lisa with passion and conviction. I was well aware that something like this could be contrived in my mind as a way to manipulate her into doing what I wanted her to do. I was careful to check my motives and make sure that God had initiated the message, not a manipulative father. As I prayerfully reevaluated the message and my motives, I knew the message was true and that it represented God's heart. I knew God desired to provide hope and encourage confidence in His care because I had experienced it in my own life.

The message renewed Lisa's willingness to be patient; it brought encouragement to her heart, giving her a perspective of faith and enabling her to trust God while waiting patiently for His work on her behalf to be completed. Three years later, God proved true to His word. He brought Lisa the man whom He had prepared especially for her.

Nurturing Faith in Your Circumstances

Faith that is alive and active and that influences your perspective and energizes your behavior does not come from religious activity or discipline. It is nurtured through relationship. The apostle Paul had this type of one-on-one relationship with God, which he describes in Galatians 2:20: "Christ lives in me; and the *life* which I now live in the flesh, I live by faith in the Son of God, who loved me and gave Himself for me."

Everyone can have this kind of faith! It is not reserved for an elite few. God has made it available to all who desire to involve Him in the daily aspects of their living.

Welcome Christ into your circumstances today and allow Him to walk with you. Give Him the authority to determine your future. He will relate to you in a personal way through the presence of the Holy Spirit, and your faith will be activated as we have discussed in this chapter. Don't wait. Welcome Him into your circumstances today.

A Concluding Thought

Faith is more than a mental consent to a set of values. It is a system of beliefs that become the motivation for action. Faith is an essential tool in our parenting partnership with God. In fact, the only way to partner with God is through faith (Hebrews 11:6).

Faith is an essential tool in our parenting partnership with God. In fact, the only way to partner with God is through faith.

Are you attempting to raise your children without a partnership between you and God? Do you possess a dynamic, interactive faith that determines perspective and influences your behavior?

Make your relationship with God intimate and personal by regularly seeking Him with all your heart. Wait expectantly on Him and search for Him with resolute determination in every situation involving you or your children. Actively apply all the promises of God's Word to your circumstances, allowing faith to orient and influence your perspective. You will witness miraculous results.

7

Components of Balanced Discipline

Part 1—Submission

True submission does not require mindless, blind loyalty
to the commands and whims of the person in charge.
True submission is revealed in the response to a person
of authority and leadership.

Lawlessness, independence, and rebellion have become behavioral norms in our society. A self-centered culture focused on "me" is swallowing up the love and self-sacrifice God intended for humanity to express toward each other. Our society's creed has become, "I want what I want when I want it, and nothing should stop me from getting it!"

The spirit of lawlessness embodied by this selfish attitude has existed upon the earth since the fall of Satan. However, it has intensified over the millennia of man's presence on earth, and it inflicts destructive havoc everywhere we look in today's society. It is a spiritual attack on God's most precious creation—humanity.

America has now produced several generations that have grown up without a model of submission and personal sacrifice. Since World War II, children have witnessed a diminishing response of corrective discipline and accountability. Schools have become hotbeds of violence. Juvenile detention centers are packed. Lawlessness, independence, and rebellion rule as never before.

Parents, government leaders, educational institutions, media conglomerates, social service organizations, and law enforcement agencies grope for solutions to these very serious and growing problems. Of course, the answer is right under their noses, but our leaders are either unwilling or unable to recognize what is needed to solve the chaos. Though readily available, the anti-virus for society's plague is ignored.

The Answer to Lawlessness

The solution is simple: we must submit to authority, embrace discipline, and allow those who love us to hold us accountable for our actions.

The solution is simple: we must submit to authority, embrace discipline, and allow those who love us to hold us accountable for our actions.

However, this solution stands in stark contrast to the prevailing mindset in America. The current mantra is that submission, discipline, and account-ability are old-fashioned, intolerant, and out of sync with modern society. "Personal responsibility" has been removed from the vocabulary of our culture. Laws are in place to make spanking a criminal offense. We substitute corrective discipline with "time-outs" in the home and society, believing distraction will somehow alter negative behavior. Using this theory, we target guns for removal so violence will diminish. We place x-ray machines at the entrances of schools, amusement parks, and sports arenas to protect partic-ipants rather than penalizing the lawless when caught. These efforts restrict the personal freedoms of the innocent rather than holding the guilty responsible for their behavior.

Once again, the principle of transference comes into play. We cannot expect our children to take responsi-bility for their behavior if we, as their parents, will not take responsibility for our own. *We cannot transfer to our children what we refuse to embrace for ourselves.* An honest examination of our hearts will reveal how deeply rooted this problem of independence and blame shifting is in the fabric of our lives! It covers a broad spectrum of behaviors, from relatively harmless mistakes to tragic errors in judgment.

When our youngest daughter, Lindsay, started driving, Jan and I decided to take advantage of the option to do parent-supervised driver education. This new program was offered to parents through the State Department of Public Service and was recognized by vehicle insurance carriers within our state.

As I gave Lindsay "in-car" driving instruction one morning, she approached an intersection coming to a stop at the corner. Lindsay made a rolling stop, quickly turning onto a street and cutting off an oncoming car. The car she cut off switched lanes and honked at her as it passed in the other lane. Lindsay was furious with the other driver for honking at her. I explained that she had cut him off in her rush to turn from the side street into traffic. Lindsay passionately objected; she did not acknowledge her error but remained upset with the other driver the rest of the way to school. In her mind, she did nothing wrong; after all, there was no accident. The other driver just had a problem. This is a simple example of the way we refuse to take responsibility for our behavior and shift the blame to someone else.

In 2013 sixteen-year-old Ethan Couch killed four people and critically injured two while driving under the influence of drugs and alcohol. He plead guilty to four counts of intoxication manslaughter and two counts of intoxication assault. The case soon gathered national attention when Couch received the surprising sentence of 10 years' probation and no jail time. His defense lawyers argued that the teenager had been so spoiled throughout his entire life that he did not understand the concepts of "right" and "wrong." His family's wealth was blamed for Couch's irresponsibility, a condition the defense lawyers named "affluenza."

This attempted justification is a sad but apt example of the lawless state of modern society. Even when wrong-doing is obvious, consequences are often minimal and, as soon proven by Couch, ineffective. In 2015 Couch and his mother fled to Mexico to avoid arrest after video evidence emerged of the now-adult Couch violating his probation. As of 2017, Couch is serving two years in prison, but his defense team continues to search for legal loopholes to reduce his sentence.

From simple mistakes to tragic errors in judgment, society's response is the same—we reject personal responsibility and deny others the right to hold us accountable.

The Subtleties of the Problem

The spirit of lawlessness has these two responses as its tap root: the unwillingness to take responsibility for behavior and the shifting of blame. Through the subtle working of these two responses, the spirit of lawlessness hypnotizes our thinking and secures its deadly hold. In subtle ways, it permeates our perspective across a broad spectrum of behaviors. Its hypnotic hold is introduced so surreptitiously that it can go almost undetected.

My dad always knew the importance of discipline in child development. He consistently administered loving correction to my sisters and me, held us accountable for our actions, and taught us to submit to authority.

When I was in junior high in the mid-1960s, the Beatles introduced their look to America's youth. I liked them, so I grew my hair "Beatles-style"—combed over my ears with long bangs.

Although I made good grades and was not a trouble-maker at school, I was called to the principal's office because my hair violated school policy. The principal told me that I could not come back to school until I cut my hair. I protested, citing my good behavior and academic record. I believed being a good student behaviorally and academically should make my hair length a non-issue. The principal did not agree, and he sent me home.

My mom was surprised to see me come home early. After I explained the situation, she dropped me off at the barbershop to get the haircut necessary to comply with the principal's demand. I told the barber I just wanted a light trim. "Don't take off too much," I said, and he willingly complied.

The next day I presented my new haircut to the principal for inspection. To my complete frustration, he sent me home again!

"I am never going back to that school!" I announced to my mom as I walked in the door. "They have no right to make me shave my head!" My interpretation was a slight exaggeration of the school's policy.

My mom allowed me to fume until my dad came home. When he arrived, I told him my side of the story. He listened patiently, nodding his head and interjecting a periodic "uh-huh," which led me to believe he agreed with me.

When I finished, he stood and motioned me toward the garage. In the garage, he motioned for me to get in the car. Then he drove me to the barbershop, walked me in, and told the barber how to cut my hair. My dad explained to me that I would submit to the authority of the school and the principal. He told me the principal's request was within the proper realm of authority, and it did not matter if we agreed. With a good attitude, we would do as the principal had asked.

Through loving correction and accountability during my childhood, my dad taught me to submit to authority. His instruction included the truth that submission is not based upon agreement.

Years later, as an adult, I saw how the lawless spirit of this age had seduced even the resolute determination of my father. One afternoon Jan and I brought Todd, who was a toddler at the time, to visit my mom and dad. We were inexperienced parents but had committed to training our children through loving discipline as our parents had trained us. This discipline included spankings, which served to get our children's attention as it taught them to obey.

As my dad and I talked in their family room that summer day, Todd became fascinated with a floor fan circulating the air in the room. Slowly and curiously, he worked his way toward the fan for a closer look. As he did, I said to him, "No, no."

The first time or two that I called him, I stood and brought him back to me, momentarily distracting his attention. Each time, however, he returned his attention to the fan. The third time I called him, he hesitated as before but then turned and proceeded toward the fan. He was old enough to understand me and had minded my "no, no's" in other situations but not this time. I stood from my chair and spanked him two times on the bottom. The process was quick; it pained his little ego more than his bottom and stopped him in his tracks. I left him in a pile of tears on the floor between the fan and my chair. I sat down again and called to him to come to me so I could comfort and love him. He sat there, his pitiful eyes looking for sympathy. In the most dramatic fashion, his eyes appealed to his grandpa, who had observed the event from the chair next to mine. Compassion arose in my dad that I could not remember from my childhood years. He looked at me and said, "We should have moved the fan. He was just curious."

I had to defend myself and remind my dad that parents should not cater to disobedience, even if it is driven by curiosity. "The fan does not need to be moved," I said. "My son needs to be trained to obey."

My dad reluctantly agreed, somehow forgetting his years of similar training that he had extended to my sisters and me.

Children learn to manipulate others and generate sympathy early in life. When Todd's appeal did not work, he responded to my encouragement, coming to me for love and assurance. He never went back to the fan.

As we later said goodbye to my parents at the door, my dad gave me a big hug and whispered in my ear, "And don't spank my grandbaby anymore!" Oh, how the roles change from parent to grandparent!

I bent down and hoisted my dad over my shoulder like a big sack of potatoes, carried him to the front yard, and twirled him around, returning him somewhat dizzy to the ground. This little demonstration between father and son reminded him that I was old enough—and strong enough—to be the dad, and I would teach my children to obey without losing my temper, as he had taught me.

My dad knew the importance of discipline in molding character in his children, yet the subtle tentacles of the spirit of lawlessness had worked their way into his thinking as he graduated from parent to grandparent. Almost imperceptibly, these tentacles attempted to change the process of discipline so necessary for equipping our next generation with the tools for success. Our playful exchange in the front yard was my effort to expose and unwrap any traces of this deception from our relationship. I wanted and expected my parents to support the work of discipline in their grandchildren.

A Three-Pronged Attack on Lawlessness

When we talk about *discipline,* we are referring to three interdependent concepts: submission, correction, and accountability.

In this chapter, we will look at the first concept, submission. In the next two chapters, we will complete the discussion with an explanation of the other two concepts. Remember, the cardinal rule in parenting is the principle of transference: you can only transfer what you have—and practice—in your own life. As we begin our look at discipline, I must ask you to scrutinize yourself as you read so you can discipline your children with the proper spirit. Another way to look at transference is to say you have as much authority to transfer the benefits of discipline to your children as you have properly responded to discipline in your own life. With this in mind, let me ask: how do *you* respond to correction? Your attitude toward submission and your response to correction will form the foundation for the training of your children.

> *Your attitude toward submission and your response to correction will form the foundation for the training of your children.*

What is Submission?

Submission is the decision to place yourself under the authority of another person or entity for correction and direction. Many equate submission with agreement. By contrast, true submission is actually revealed in disagreement. *True submission does not require mindless or blind obedience to the commands and whims of the person in charge.* True submission is revealed in one's response to authority and leadership.

It is impossible to understand and walk in submission fully without the knowledge of and confidence in God's sovereignty. Men will fail in leadership positions; they will operate with impure motives that hurt and abuse others; they will make unintentional mistakes that bring painful consequences. Our submission, then, is not first and foremost to men. It is to God, who works through imperfect men to reveal and produce His will and to protect those submitted to Him.

I submit to those in authority over me because the Bible says God placed them there. Romans 13:1–2 says:

> Let every soul be subject to the governing authorities. For there is no authority except from God, and the authorities that exist are appointed by God. Therefore whoever resists the authority resists the ordinance of God, and those who resist will bring judgment on themselves.

Our superiors are worthy of respect due to God's appointment and placement of them, not because they have earned our seal of approval. Of course, we should only submit to direction that is legal, moral, and agrees with God's law. In my life, most of the difficult situations that arise requiring my submission meet those criteria. The only situation in my adult experience that would have justified resistance to submission is the situation I described in the last chapter. It involved a scenario where my boss asked me to lie in placing an order for a customer. Since it involved a state contract, I felt his request compromised my integrity and put me in potential legal jeopardy. I determined I would not comply with his request, even if it cost me my job.

Almost every situation requiring submission becomes a battle of the mind. When faced with such situations, I find myself attempting to categorize every situation as illegal, immoral, or in disagreement with God's law so that I can do what I want rather than properly submit.

I know what I am saying is difficult, and I've struggled to get this right at times. But when I fail, I always find myself in the middle of correction by God's hand. One such instance occurred as I fulfilled my duties as a pastor. Our church had been in a constant state of growth. From our beginning in 1978, we grew to over 7,000 members, and the ministries of the church had far-reaching influence. During one growth spurt, we needed expanded facilities for our youth. We found a vacant Quonset-style steel building once used as a roller-skating rink. We leased it and began remodeling the interior to serve the needs of our youth. I supervised the project, providing direct oversight to the project manager who was a paid staff member of the church.

As with many construction projects, this one involved some unforeseen work, and in the finishing stages, it was over budget and past the completion deadline. For several weeks in a row, our senior pastor, who was my boss, directed me to bring the project to completion. He instructed me to finish the work in process and to delay anything not already begun.

However, new "mini projects" kept developing that took their place in the line of items required to bring the project to completion. Each week, I explained to my boss why the project had not been completed, providing him with details of the mini projects. Each week, he instructed me to finish and not start any new projects. After several weeks of this back-and-forth, my work was brought into question. I justified the extension of the project with this attitude: if my boss were responsible for the work, he would understand that the mini-projects were necessary to bring the full project to completion.

The project was eventually brought to completion. However, at my year-end review, I was corrected, and my salary increase for the next year was adjusted. I felt the correction was unfair; I felt I had been misunderstood. As others in leadership became aware of my correction, I was embarrassed. I felt if I could explain myself in full detail, telling about the importance of the mini projects, all would be able to see that I was not the problem. The project was the problem!

My pride was hurt, and I mentally began the justification for my actions, even giving thought to resigning. I thought about gathering a few of those close to me who held positions of influence to plead my case. As I contemplated my options, the Lord broke into my consciousness and spoke to my heart. He clearly asked, "Are you going to let Me correct you?"

"Yes, Lord," I said immediately. "But You know all the details about the mini projects. Surely You understand correction is not needed."

God continued, "Then receive this correction and submit to the authority I have placed over you, and do it with a good attitude! You did *not* do as you were directed; you were rebellious in your heart to the direction of your boss. No excuses." "Yes, Lord, I receive your correction. I am sorry," was my response.

I chose this example to present two important concepts related to submission. The first is that *everyone, regardless of age or responsibility, is under someone else's authority—yes, everyone!* Authority in our lives is as sure as death and taxes. The questions we must answer are: How will we relate and respond to authority? Will we submit, or will our actions be independent and rebellious?

Second, *if we do not submit to God's appointed earthly authority, then we will not submit to God either.* Remember what Romans 13:2 says: "Therefore whoever resists the authority resists the ordinance of God, and those who resist will bring judgment on themselves."

If we do not submit to God's
appointed earthly authority, then we
will not submit to God either.

Some who claim to love God and serve Him are rebellious. They act independently of His appointed authority in their lives. Our response to earthly authority, whether one of submission or rebellious independence, is our response to God's authority. It does not matter how our mind might justify our actions; rebellious independence is wrong. However, a submitted response pleases God and brings His favor (1 Peter 2:18).

A Concluding Thought

Submission is a critical concept for living. It forms the foundation for God's work and blessing in our lives. In this chapter, has the Lord revealed some action or attitude related to submission in your life? Perhaps you have recognized that your father's discipline was negligent, that it fostered lawlessness in your attitude toward submission. Or perhaps you have gained a new understanding related to the concepts of submission and the connective foundation it provides for the whole structure of discipline.

As God brings enlightenment to you, it is important to make the appropriate response to Him. Repent for any acts of rebellion or independence. If specific instances come to mind, simply acknowledge your behavior or attitude as wrong.

Commit today to live in submission to all authority in your life—your government, employer, pastor, and parents. Become accountable to an individual or a group of men who love God and will love you.

You may feel discomfort at first as you make changes in your life, but don't allow negative feelings or thoughts to stop you from taking action. Your response will bring blessing to your life and change your whole approach to corrective discipline, forming the foundation for understanding and the authority to bring proper correction to your children.

8

Components of Balanced Discipline

Part 2—Correction

God's motive for correction is love.
His reason is always redemptive.

I n the previous chapter, we discussed the importance
of submission as the first of three interdependent
concepts of discipline: submission, correction, and
accountability.

Without a proper understanding of each, the Bible's
presentation of discipline cannot be fully understood. To
emphasize one concept over the others or to exclude one
in favor of another will produce imbalanced and ineffective training for our children.

Now we will examine the next concept: *correction.*
Keep two things in mind as you read this chapter:

First, God has made men the managers of their
homes (see 1 Corinthians 11:3). Therefore, He will
hold them responsible for establishing a standard of
values and implementing them in a manner consistent
with His nature. Jesus reveals this principle in the

parable of a certain rich man (representing God) who
entrusted his possessions to a manager (representing
us). The rich man later learned that his manager was
wasting these possessions. He called the manager and
demanded, "What is this I hear about you? Get your
report in order, because you are going to be fired"
(Luke 16:2 NLT).

As the leaders and managers of their homes, men will
be called to give an account of how they managed their
families. Therefore, we must set the parameters for
appropriate behavior, model it in our lives, and work to
transfer it graciously to our children. Our reaction or
indifference to issues that confront our family members
will have a dramatic influence on the future atmosphere
in our home, along with influencing the behavior of each
member of our family.

Many men leave the responsibility for correction
to their wives. In doing so, these fathers shirk their
God-given responsibility to lead their families and miss
the opportunity to be the influence God intended them
to be.

Second, remember the principle of transference. As
you read this chapter, take some time to scrutinize your
actions before attempting to influence your children's
behavior through discipline. Remember—you must
model the standard before you can transfer it to your
children.

The Purpose of Correction

God's motive for correction is love. His reason is always redemptive. He disciplines us to rescue us from a terrible fate, as He knows that sin snowballs over time into an avalanche of misery. Therefore, God's correction is always a blessing. Though painful for the moment, it is administered with a long-term perspective in mind.

> *God's correction is always a blessing.*
> *Though painful for the moment, it*
> *is administered with a long-term*
> *perspective in mind.*

Many parents lose or never even have this perspective when correcting their children. Their correction becomes motivated by something other than the future result of their children's behavior. Instead, their motivation is anger, frustration, embarrassment, impatience, or inconvenience. The emotion created by their children's behavior leads to an effort to establish authority, demonstrate power, or maintain control. *When parents allow pride, ego, authority, or position to motivate correction, they miss its real purpose.* As a result, the correction becomes abusive and harsh.

The most important function of a father is to demonstrate the nature and character of God to his wife and children. As fathers, we obviously cannot measure up to God's perfect nature, but if we make an honest effort to do so, His grace covers our shortcomings. Combined with our diligent efforts, His help will establish a gracious standard, correct wrong behavior, and transfer His nature, instead of our imperfections, to our children.

What Method of Correction Is Appropriate?

A variety of correction methods are effective. The situation should determine the specific method used to bring correction. Consider God's correction. He is patient and always kind. He is quick to forgive, never withdrawing relationship when we acknowledge our rebellion and disobedience, ask for forgiveness, and change our attitude or behavior. The method we use to bring correction to our children should represent God's manner of bringing correction to us.

IS SPANKING APPROPRIATE?

I realize spanking is quite controversial as a method of correction. Society today frowns upon spanking for two reasons. First, it is often used only to punish rather than to correct. There is a significant difference between the two. Second, the current prevailing thought is that humanity's intelligence has progressed so much that it has surpassed the wisdom of the Bible.

It no longer recognizes the authority of statements like Proverbs 13:24:

> He who spares his rod hates his son,
> But he who loves him disciplines him promptly.

Spanking is thought of by some as harsh, punitive, and almost barbaric. I strongly disagree with this perspective. Spanking should never be done in an abusive manner. If it is administered wrongly, it can be damaging. However, I will show that when done correctly, spanking can be used to produce correction. I will also give the specific steps that must be taken to guard against abuse.

Jan and I used spanking to train our children. Spanking creates an association in our children's minds between pain and disobedience. My firm belief is that a spanking applied to the padded part of a child's bottom produces pain without physical or emotional damage. The pain helps teach children two important concepts necessary for correction to be effective:

1. It teaches them to recognize that obedience is a choice.
2. It teaches them to associate disobedience with painful consequences.

When done correctly, spanking develops a sense of responsibility in children for their actions. Their young instincts take over, and self-preservation encourages obedience.

When our children were old enough to understand "no," we began spanking them when they disobeyed. At first, we used a pat on the hand to correct them for touching or grabbing something against our instruction. When this was no longer effective, Jan or I gave a "swat" by our hand on their diaper-covered bottom. As our children grew, the day came when a swat by our hand failed to accomplish the correction we sought. The next step was to spank them with a wooden spoon or paddle. Never did we swat or spank on the legs or upper body—only on the bottom.

Your child's reaction will help identify the type of spanking method to use and when to change to a new method. A steely-eyed defiance that tells you "that didn't hurt" is the indication it is time to make a change in your method.

When we spanked our children, we always followed the same routine. Inconsistency is the enemy of discipline, so we always followed these four steps without compromise or wavering.

Do not spank in anger

If we were angry or frustrated, we sent our child to the bedroom to wait for us. This gave them time to consider their behavior and gave us time to take a deep breath and regain our composure before correcting them.

Spank in private

Correction is a private matter and should never be used to embarrass a child. As such, we never spanked our children in front of friends, siblings, other adults, or in a public place.

Explain the offense before spanking

In the privacy of a bedroom or other secluded place, we always asked our children to tell us the reason they were getting a spanking. Almost without fail, the response was, "I don't know." We learned that a child must understand the reason behind the discipline for the correction to have the proper influence on his behavior. A brief explanation from them will reveal their level of understanding. If a child cannot explain what he did wrong, we must explain the unacceptable behavior in a way he can understand.

Administer pain, not abuse

The purpose of spanking is to help our children associate disobedience with pain, not to create fear in them. Pain by itself does not produce correction, especially when the motive is self-serving to the parent. Spanking out of anger or frustration, or on places other than the padded part of a child's bottom, does not produce the corrective result we are seeking, and it risks injury to the child. The result is physical abuse, which is the direct opposite of God's intended purpose. *Any parent who physically damages a child and thinks the punishment will change his behavior does not understand God's view of correction.*

> *The purpose of spanking is to help our children associate disobedience with pain, not to create fear in them.*

If these steps are followed, your children will not cower in your presence, nor fear your wrath, but they will learn to respond obediently to your direction.

THE RESPONSES WE WANT FROM OUR CHILDREN

In addition to following the above steps when disciplining our children, Jan and I also required these three responses from them:

Be able to explain the offense

As stated above, we wanted our children to explain in their own words how they disobeyed. Disobedience was always the reason for correction. We needed to know that our children knew what part of their behavior disobeyed our instruction. They were not allowed to be mad at us or go silent in response to our correction.

Show genuine sorrow for disobedience

One important way children indicate sorrow is the attitude with which they receive correction. We wanted our children to understand that our motive for correction was the same as God's motive: our love for them. Before correction, we reminded our children that we did not let them disobey because of our love for them. We told them that by learning to obey us, they learned to obey God. It was important for them to learn to obey so that when they left home and had families of their own, they would obey God and live under His authority.

Accept affection from the parent who spanked them

After the spanking, we allowed the child to have a short time of demonstrative response to ease the pain. This included crying, holding one's bottom, or dropping to the floor in a pile of emotions. However, we didn't allow the response to be prolonged, overly dramatic, or an angry display of aggression toward us. Finally, the correction was not complete until our child accepted physical and emotional comfort from the disciplining parent. The comfort usually consisted of a hug and/or kiss between both parties.

On occasion, our children refused to come for love and comfort to the disciplining parent. Instead, they

looked to the non-disciplining parent. When pride has
suffered a blow, it is natural to be defiant, to reject
the person bringing the correction, and to have a
bad attitude about the whole process. Nevertheless,
our response was always the same: We would wait
and insist on the giving and acceptance of love. We
would not leave the place of correction until love was
demonstrated.

If one step in the process of correction is missed more
often than any other, it is the step of affection. When
anger or frustration has been the catalyst for the correction, rejection is the easiest response to reinforce our
displeasure. Thus, children are spanked, sent to their
rooms, or allowed to walk away in shame. We must avoid
this response.

Jan and I never ignored or eliminated the step of
affection, nor did we tell our children to "go to your
bedroom to think about what you have done," which
would only serve to shame them for unacceptable
behavior. *Shame does not produce correct behavior.* A
spanking—not shame, not rejection—is the penalty for
disobedience.

When the three-step process was completed, all was
forgiven, and we walked forward without pointing to or
constantly referring back to the correction as a reminder
of their failure. The Bible tells us that when we receive
God's correction, He removes our sin as far as the east

is from the west (Psalm 103:12). God doesn't use our failures to condemn and reject us, so we should not do that to our children either.

> *God doesn't use our failures to*
> *condemn and reject us, so we should*
> *not do that to our children either.*

WHAT ABOUT TIME-OUTS, GROUNDING, AND OTHER DIVERSIONS?

Many parents use time-outs as a replacement for spanking during their children's pre-teen years. While spanking is not the only method of correction parents have at their disposal, it should not be replaced or eliminated in favor of other methods like time-outs. Proverbs 13:24, mentioned earlier in this chapter, is still valid for this age group. Spanking in their pre-teen years teaches children responsibility for their actions and greatly reduces discipline problems in their teenage years.

I believe the use of a time-out can be effective when young children become so frenzied they are not paying attention to instructions. Used in this manner, a time-out gives children the opportunity to think more clearly, stop their activity, and listen and respond from a more rational state. It allows them the opportunity to choose to obey. When used in this manner, a time-out can be an effective intervening step before a spanking is administered. It gives children a chance to slow down, pay attention, and change their behavior. However, if they fail to take advantage of this cautionary step, they need to be spanked. A further time-out will not produce the needed correction.

Correcting Teenagers

In their early teenage years, our children reached a physical size that made spanking almost impossible and, in reality, no longer effective. We still administered correction, but at this age, we found that removing privileges more effectively reinforced our correction. As children move into their teenage years, something I call the "Timex Factor" happens. Like the famous watch, they can "take a lickin' and keep on tickin'!"

Grounding (or withholding privileges) administers a pain more effective than spanking for this age group. It involves denying the teenager a privilege such as being with friends, talking on the phone, using the Internet, driving, or attending special events.

Parents must be careful in the way they administer grounding because this method needs to be tailored to the specific personality and interests of each child. What is effective for one child will be wasted upon another. The duration and frequency must be considered carefully. Used improperly, grounding can quickly lose its corrective benefit and become a greater punishment to parents than to their children! When this happens, parents become inconsistent in enforcing the grounding, and the corrective benefit is lost. Teenagers quickly learn that the grounding doesn't stick, and they develop an attitude of indifference, even defiance, toward this form of correction.

Attitudes Are the Seeds of Behavior

Jesus' parables often emphasized that a person's actions originate from thoughts (Matthew 15:19). This is a powerful truth. The process of thoughts leading to behavior is what psychologists call "acting out." Jesus taught that we are ultimately what we think, and He encouraged His followers to guard their thoughts carefully.

Attitudes reside in our hearts and influence our thinking. Our thinking determines our behavior. Therefore, we must correct both behavior and attitudes. Correcting an attitude will expose a problem before it becomes a behavioral pattern.

Correcting an attitude will expose
a problem before it becomes
a behavioral pattern.

Our third child, Tyler, was a fun, funny, easy-going child, with an intense loyalty and a strong sense of fairness. Tyler was so adaptable that we often wouldn't know the strength of his feelings or opinions. When he was in the third grade, we transferred Tyler, along with his older sister, Lisa, to a private Christian school.

During the first two weeks at the new school, Tyler complained that the school rules were unfair. For example, the school instructed children to keep their hands to themselves. Children were not allowed to run their hands along the hall walls, bother other people, or touch things that were not theirs. Dress codes and other rules were strictly enforced.

One day, Tyler came home and announced that he had encountered the most ridiculous and unreasonable rule yet. In fact, this rule was so unfair that he wanted out of "that crummy school." I could hardly wait to hear what was so unreasonable.

"One of my friends got swats for yawning in class!" he told me. "Yawning in class, Dad! Can you believe that?" I quizzed him a little further, quite certain he might have overlooked an important detail or two. "Well," Tyler responded, "the teacher did tell him to cover his mouth when he yawned. But come on, Dad. Is that ridiculous or what?"

As he responded, it dawned on me that Tyler had an attitude of independence. He didn't like someone telling him or his friend what to do. In the public school system, Tyler's attitude of independence had gone unchallenged. Standards of behavior were different, and teachers had more kids to monitor than the teachers in the private school did. Under tighter controls and a smaller student-teacher ratio, Tyler's independent attitude popped out.

Over the years of my pastoral ministry, I have had the opportunity to know many families and watch them mature. I have been able to watch children develop from birth through adulthood. One young man came into the world with an attitude. He was cranky and fussy as a baby, and even in happy times, he was demanding.

As a toddler, he was rough with his toys and his friends, never treating them with respect or care. His rough attitude and behavior carried across all stages of his development. When something broke due to his lack of care or abuse, he expected his parents to get it fixed or replace it immediately. He was hard to live with until his desire was fulfilled. You might say he was spoiled!

I was puzzled as I watched how his parents reacted to his behavior. From preschool through his early twenties, they coddled his behavior and selfish attitudes, making excuses like: "We kept him up past his nap time"; "He hasn't been feeling well"; and "This has been a rough week for him." They rarely addressed or corrected his attitude or behavior.

When this boy was in his upper teens, he and some friends took the family boat out to the lake for a day of fun. The boys started doing some dangerous stunts involving the boat. During one of the stunts, they hit something submerged in the water, knocking a hole in the boat. It took on water and quickly sank. None of the boys were seriously injured in the mishap. The young man whose parents owned the boat turned to his friends and said, "Don't worry, my parents will get me a new boat!"

Where do you suppose he got that attitude? It was developed and nurtured in him from the time he was an infant. Little things will become big issues with potentially devastating consequences if they go unchecked.

I knew if Tyler's response to the school rules went unchecked and if I failed to address his seemingly harmless attitude right then and there, it would lead to further reactions of resistance and independence. My failure to act when this attitude was seemingly harmless would have opened the door to rebellious behavior later in his life. I was thankful to catch it in seed form and deal with it as an attitude before it grew to produce behavior that would be difficult to control or have potentially devastating consequences.

A Concluding Thought

Hurts and judgments from childhood prevent many adults from finding balance in the whole concept of discipline, especially as it relates to spanking, time-outs, and grounding.

Many adults who were reared in harsh, dominant, or controlling environments that included physical or verbal abuse promised themselves that they would never treat their children the same way. This inner promise often results in an extreme type of parenting. At one end of the scale is a parent who struggles to administer discipline and ends up not disciplining at all. The result is out-of-control behavior in their children. On the other end of the scale are parents who abuse their children with hands or words and end up hating themselves for becoming just like their parents!

This kind of response is called an "inner vow," a personal promise formed from a judgment that lives in our hearts and works itself out in our lives. It is often revealed in statements such as "I will never ..." or "I will always ..." Like a computer virus that corrupts a hard drive and contaminates files, altering the ability of a computer to operate properly, inner vows infect hearts and spirits. They prevent us from obeying God and keep us from implementing the truths we have received. An inner vow will prevent you from finding the proper balance in your responses to your children.

To be free from an inner vow, you must forgive the person responsible for creating your pain, and you must renounce the vow you have made. This will open the door for you to ask God to forgive and heal you. Only then will you be able to train and correct your children properly.

This does not have to be an elaborate prayer. Just tell God that you forgive those who hurt you and ask for His healing touch in your life. There is tremendous power in speaking out loud, and it is important that you hear yourself forgive them.

Next, ask God to enable you to be an influential parent who properly understands and applies discipline to correct disobedient behavior. God will hear your prayer, and He will respond!

9

Components of Balanced Discipline

Part 3—Accountability

Accountability involves submitting to a limited number of individuals whose primary motivation involves your best interests and the fulfillment of God's will for your life.

Applying discipline without accountability is like buying a shiny new car and never checking the engine fluids once you leave the dealer's lot. Everything will work wonderfully for a while, but without oil, antifreeze, and hydraulic fluid, something will seize up, causing major damage that could easily have been avoided! Just as a car needs the right engine fluids to operate properly, discipline needs all three of its components—submission, correction, and accountability—to operate as God intended.

In this chapter, we will discuss the final element: accountability. Accountability plays an important support role to the other two elements by protecting and reinforcing the lessons they teach. Without accountability, the instruction of discipline is quickly forgotten, and its ability to influence and shape future behavior is lost.

What is Accountability?

Accountability is a term that evokes negative feelings from most men. Many would define accountability as a relationship between two individuals in which one person dominates or controls the other. Real accountability, though, is not dominating or controlling at all. It is supportive and protective.

Accountability is submission to an individual or small group based on a relationship of love and care. A person who chooses to be accountable extends an open invitation to a select few to influence his life, allowing them to review behavior and thoughts, give input, and express concerns.

Accountability invites honest and caring input. Through relational care, accountability exposes blind spots and directs action away from harmful behavior or circumstances. It draws on another person's experience, wisdom, or knowledge of God and His ways to confirm direction, help fashion a well-thought-out strategy, or shape a response to weak areas of temptation.

> *Through relational care,*
> *accountability exposes blind spots*
> *and directs action away from harmful*
> *behavior or circumstances.*

Mechanisms of accountability establish a platform for mentoring. Mentoring is a process in which one person's knowledge and experience are used to shape, influence, and benefit another. Accountability establishes a very important relationship between two individuals and must be treated with respect by both parties. The requirements to be an effective mentor are the same requirements needed to be an effective father:

- A mentor should love God openly.
- A mentor should know and love you unconditionally.
- A mentor should earnestly desire to see God's will and blessings manifest in your life.

The most logical person to fulfill the duties of a mentor is a father. Who better? Who more qualified? It just makes sense that no person could be a better mentor to you than your father. Unfortunately, very few men have this type of relationship with their fathers. Most men do not have any real accountability in their lives. I know of some who have sought accountability but struggled to find a man who had a clue about how to mentor them or what accountability was all about.

An accountability crisis has developed in modern culture because we have been encouraged to be self-sufficient, producing an independence that has perverted the implementation of accountability among today's men. This lack of accountability has produced devastating consequences in our personal lives as well as in our families.

God is always merciful to raise a voice of instruction when a truth or principle is being ignored. The Promise Keepers ministry, founded by Coach Bill McCartney, was one such voice during the 1990s. It became God's standard bearer to teach men the truth about accountability and call them out of independence and self-sufficiency.

Accountable relationships bless us by enabling us to make good decisions and preparing us to act right and lead our families in healthy ways. Unfortunately, most men have never seen or experienced accountability and have no idea how to practice it with their children—and once again, a man cannot transfer what he does not have.

How Does Accountability Work?

The purpose of accountability is to enable you to make wise decisions in your life. It begins with an attitude of submission, which at its core is a willingness to present issues for review or consideration before they are finalized or acted upon. *The final decision is never the mentor's; it always remains with the individual who has to live with the outcome.*

Accountability simply adds wisdom, experience, and an objective perspective to the decision-making process, making it possible to avoid costly mistakes. It is not surrendering a decision to any random person you meet who might offer an opinion. It involves submitting to a limited number of individuals whose primary motivation involves your best interests and the fulfillment of God's will for your life.

> *The purpose of accountability*
> *is to enable you to make wise decisions*
> *in your life. It begins with an attitude*
> *of submission.*

Bad decisions may result from several things: overwhelmingly strong desires; confusion caused by too many options; "roller coaster" emotions that lead us through euphoric and depressive swings. Accountability protects us from the influences that cause bad decisions. A mentor provides a stable, objective perspective to help sort out the confusion of emotions and desires. His input provides safety and presents the best possibility of success through the maze of life's options and varied circumstances.

Establishing the Foundation for Accountability

Accountability draws upon three qualities associated with humility: openness, honesty, and the ability to receive correction. Men have difficulty showing these important qualities because they think it makes them look weak; however, these traits are critical for accountability.

The first quality is openness. No human can be present to monitor our thoughts and actions 24 hours a day, 7 days a week. We must be willing to discuss our thoughts, feelings, and behaviors. We must be open regarding the issues that cause pressure or unrest and lead us to wrongdoing.

The second quality is honesty. We must be willing to explain our behaviors truthfully and fully disclose, as much as we are aware, our reasons, thoughts, and intentions. Hiding feelings, thoughts, or behaviors defeats the purpose and work of accountability.

The third quality is the ability to receive correction. Through the trust we have with our mentors, we must be willing to allow them to confront us for misbehavior. We must listen and carefully weigh their objective perspectives on the issues in our lives, factoring them into our actions. We cannot withdraw from correction by becoming defensive or angry. We must be able to rest in the trust we have in our mentors, knowing that they are truly concerned with God's will and blessings for our life.

Accountability is as much an attitude as it is an action. Accountability must be extended from one person to another whom they know, trust, and respect. It is done voluntarily, not by force. You cannot be an effective mentor for your children until you first have made yourself accountable. You should seek and embrace accountability for its benefits in your own life, but if this is not enough incentive, then do it for your children. Remember, the principle of transference is the hub of all other parenting principles but especially the principle of accountability. Take action today to make sure this principle is active in your life for the benefit of your children!

> *You cannot be an effective mentor for your children until you first have made yourself accountable.*

The Father's Role as Mentor

A mentor is not simply a good friend. A relationship of accountability deepens the friendship through a foundation of trust and molds the inner fabric of the person being mentored. While it is true that a friend can provide a listening ear, serve as a sounding board, extend comfort, and offer free advice, a mentoring relationship goes much deeper. A mentor is trusted to give knowledgeable and loving advice and to monitor behaviors and attitudes throughout the circumstances of life. Trust enables the person being mentored to act on the mentor's advice in the immediate circumstance, whether it makes sense or not. This is not blind trust extended to a self-serving, controlling person who is casually involved in your life. Instead, it is trust based on a relationship that has no demands or strings attached. A mentor must make a significant, long-term commitment; he must draw on his experiences in life to guide and benefit the person under his care.

A mentoring relationship with your children has its fullest expression as they mature. However, as with all aspects of parenting, you cannot wait to begin until they are approaching their adult years. Your work begins the day you bring them home from the hospital. A father cannot simply be a friend to his child; he is a trainer, advisor, and experienced liver of life who teaches his apprentice what he needs to know to succeed.

A father cannot simply be a friend to his child; he is a trainer, advisor, and experienced liver of life who teaches his apprentice what he needs to know to succeed.

Until my dad passed away in 1989, he was a mentor to me. He influenced every significant event in my life. I am fortunate to have enjoyed a similar relationship with my father-in-law as well. Over the years, these mentors gave me wise counsel and saved me from many choices that would have brought certain disaster.

When I was in elementary school, my dad influenced me in many ways: through our involvement in athletics and YMCA Indian Guides; by his example in business and leisure; and especially in the way he treated my mom and my sisters. During my teenage years, my dad taught me to drive, set parameters for dating, monitored my homework and school activities, and instilled important life values necessary for family and business success. When I became an adult, my dad guided me through major purchase decisions, career changes, and other transitions in life.

My dad and my father-in-law met the three-fold requirement for mentors mentioned above. They imparted wisdom and gave advice on the significant decisions related to my life and family without dominating or controlling my behavior. Some men resist accountability because they have only experienced dominating or controlling relationships. They have never experienced a relationship in which input and advice were given solely for their good.

Because I experienced this positive input from my dad and my father-in-law, I had a model to draw from as my children matured. My dad was never controlling, manipulative, or dominating, so my relationship with my children has never been that way either.

An Example of Accountability

When I became an adult, I made the conscious choice to continue to allow my dad to mentor me. It required an active decision on my part to be open, honest, and correctable. The result was that my dad protected me from costly mistakes that would have damaged my finances and my family.

One such incident took place in the first year of my marriage. We were living in our hometown of Omaha, Nebraska, in an apartment on a shoestring budget. I attended school and worked part-time. Jan was essentially the breadwinner, working full-time and providing the main financial support for our family.

One day a good friend of mine offered to sell me his 1950 army surplus jeep, which had been sitting in storage for several years while he served in Vietnam. Although I was not a proficient mechanic, I always had a dream of rebuilding a classic car. Of course, the jeep was not a classic car, but in my mind's eye, I could see it fully restored with a new paint job, super-charged engine, fancy wheels, new interior, and a soft top. The jeep had not been started in over two years, but I remembered how it ran. I could see in my imagination the smooth-running power of the new 327-cubic inch engine I was going to put under the hood. It was going to be cool!

At that moment, though, it did not look too great. Its four coats of paint were peeling. Oh, and there was one other minor problem—my friend could not find the key. But to me, this only added excitement to my feelings of anticipation. It meant the first step toward restoration was a new ignition switch!

Do I even need to say Jan did not share my enthusiasm? She had not yet caught the vision of what this ugly mass of metal was going to become. However, with a little persuasion, she saw the light and gave me her cautious okay to buy the jeep.

Since Jan and I lived in an apartment, my parents allowed me to use their garage for the project. The four of us had dinner together, and then my friend and I towed the jeep back to my parents' house and pushed it into the garage. I was so proud of our work up to that point.

Jan came out for an inspection. She immediately burst into tears and went running back into the house. It was worse than she had expected.

I was unfazed by her emotions. I knew she would come around as the restoration began to take shape. I was confident she would share my joy on the great day we rolled my shiny hot rod—the coolest jeep in the world—out of the garage for her maiden trip.

As I said goodbye to my friend, my dad came out for an inspection. I excitedly began to share my dream with him, describing in detail how I would restore this "beast" to glory. I felt it was a good, manly term to describe this future beauty in her current state. Without a word, my dad circled the "beast," kicking the tires and inspecting the rust spots.

"So, what do you think, Dad?" I asked, certain he would share my excitement.

"Well, son," he said slowly, "You're an adult, and you're married, so this is between you and your wife. If you decide to do this, you are welcome to use the garage."

I needed more. I needed his encouragement and support. I wanted him to share the vision. "Yeah, yeah, thanks, Dad," I said, motioning with my arm. "But what do you think?"

And then my dad did something really great. He told me the truth.

"What do I think?" he asked. "This is how I size up your situation, son: your wife is in the house crying, and this pile of junk is not a restoration project. It is a complete rebuild, a rolling sinkhole that will suck up dollars. Furthermore, what you are planning to do in restoring this worthless excuse for transportation will cost big dollars, which you don't have at this time in your life."

He paused, pondering his next statement, then continued. "You can do this if you want, but if you do, I am going to think you're stupid!" Talk about a wet blanket on my vision!

I was blinded to the reality of my situation and needed a jolt back to reality. I needed the words of my mentor. Although my dad spoke sharply, I had learned from childhood to trust him; he was always interested in my success. His love for me propelled him to tell me the truth, and it opened my eyes to reality.

I sold the jeep the next day to a guy who worked at the plumbing supply house where I traded, and that ended my restoration project.

A mentor will often see the facts clearly while you are blinded by circumstances, as I was in this situation. My dad still respected my right to make the decision, but the strength of his view opened my eyes to the folly of my fantasy. I avoided a costly mistake, one that would have taken money we didn't have—but more importantly, he helped me avoid deeply damaging my relationship with Jan through selfish insensitivity. My attitude of submission to my dad allowed me to reap the good results of accountability.

I carried the principles of accountability into adulthood, and as a father, I have taught them to my children. Todd, my oldest son, is now married with a family and a career. In 1999, when he had worked for the same employer for five years, another job opportunity came his way. A large pharmaceutical company offered him a lucrative sales territory in a small West Texas town. Within days of this unsolicited offer, his company offered him a transfer to a new assignment in New Zealand.

Both opportunities had positive and negative aspects for Todd and his wife. In the process of making his decision, Todd called on me as his father and mentor and presented me with both opportunities. He openly discussed what he saw as the positives and negatives of the two offers and then asked for my perspective and advice.

A mentor is not free to impose his will on the person with whom he is in relationship. He must draw on his knowledge of God and his personal experience to offer counsel that will further God's purpose in his mentee's life.

One offer would give Todd international business experience before he was thirty years old. The other offer would give him future promotion possibilities and good training, but it would also put him in an obscure town in West Texas. The fatherly side of me selfishly wanted to advise Todd to take the latter option. It would have placed him just three hours from us and two hours from his wife's family.

As we talked, I felt the best offer for Todd and his future involved a move to New Zealand. Todd agreed but thought it was a huge step for him and his young family. I assured him that God would provide friends for them and establish them just as He would if they were relocating within the United States. With our encouragement and support, Todd and Blynda moved to New Zealand.

It was God's plan for them and one of the best experiences of their lives. It bolstered Todd's business career and gave him and his wife a picture of God's power and work all across the world. It enabled them to make friends they will have for a lifetime. While they were there, they had their first child, Olivia, who now has dual citizenship in the United States and New Zealand.

Todd and his wife did not decide to move to New Zealand on their own but received sensitive input from multiple mentors who confirmed God's work and His next step in their lives. What a powerful blessing accountability is!

A Concluding Thought

As a father, your decision to be accountable will bring blessing and protection to you and your family. If you need someone to be accountable to, ask God to help you find a mentor who meets the three-fold requirement we have discussed. Your mentor might be a pastor, a Bible study leader, an older man in your life, a trusted friend, your father, or your father-in-law.

Why not take action and change your life today? Cast off independence, self-sufficiency, and pride. Submit your life to someone who cares for you, beginning with God. He is your best friend. He will honor your decision, provide you a mentor, and bring blessing and protection to your life. Your decision will also enable you to teach your children about accountability and prepare you to be a mentor to them, a benefit that will touch and influence multiple generations.

10

Using the Experiences of Life as Your Classroom

Children need to learn how to extract benefit from every
circumstance before they leave home. They will use this
important skill throughout their adult lives.,

Most concepts essential for living as God designed
are not learned through classroom instruction—
things such as commitment, diligence, and honoring
your word. My dad knew this, so he instilled these traits
in me by encouraging me to use the situations of life as
my laboratory for application and discovery.

I do not remember my dad ever teaching me his values
through formal instruction. He sometimes weaved
principles into our conversation at the dinner table,
but the practical application of them was always taught
and reinforced in the classroom of life. Even though as
parents we do not know what tomorrow will bring, we
can be assured that opportunities will develop on a daily
basis to teach and impart God's principles for living to
our children. Opportunities must be recognized and

applied correctly for the training to have its maximum benefit.

When I was a boy, my dad modeled his values for me by allowing me to watch as he confronted everyday life situations, applying his values to determine his response and shape the outcome. He also monitored my life and involved himself so he could identify circumstances that were impacting me and use them to show me how to apply his principles to formulate my response. The focus of his concern was never the details of the circumstances; he was concerned with the principle to be imparted or the lesson to be learned. Using life's circumstances, he taught me to turn "lemons into lemonade," making the most of events by turning them into cases for study and instruction in the laboratory of life. In this way, he drove home such principles as commitment, diligence, and the priority of honoring my word.

The Correct View of Circumstances

As I have come to understand the sovereignty of God, I see His work expressed in the circumstances that arise in my life. This view has allowed me to recognize events for what they truly are: *times for God to teach me and impart principles necessary to fulfill some aspect of His plan for my life.*

God is always present. He is more powerful than any situation confronting me, and He has all knowledge; no matter how challenging the events are to me, they are no challenge to Him. This understanding of God's sovereignty has enabled me to view events and circumstances from the perspective of God's involvement in them and the ultimate good He is out to achieve.

It helps me to realize that every issue coming into my life must pass God's approval process. Nothing is the result of bad luck or under the control of entities seeking my harm. When circumstances come my way that are difficult, unfair, or the opposite of what I desire, I find comfort in the knowledge that God is in control.

> *Every issue coming into my life must pass God's approval process. Nothing is the result of bad luck or under the control of entities seeking my harm.*

God promises to use the circumstances of our lives to accomplish His good work. As parents, we must use circumstances to train and instruct our children, thus building a framework for their understanding and accepting of God's work as it carries on throughout their lives.

Using Circumstances to Instruct and Impart Life Principles

Our two boys, Todd and Tyler, are six years apart. In their early years, Tyler was always Todd's "pesky" little brother. As they matured, a friendship developed that now reflects a deep love and brotherly respect. However, during their years at home, many situations provided teaching opportunities for me to impart lasting principles.

When Todd was about 16 and Tyler was 10—still in the "pesky" little brother stage—a situation occurred that exposed two flaws in the attitudes of my boys, giving me the opportunity to train them and impart my family values to them.

Todd's best friend, Kyle, called to invite Todd over to his house. When Tyler heard what his big brother was doing, he asked if he could go with Todd to play with Kyle's younger brother, Collier. Like ours, Kyle's family had four children, and his younger brother, Collier, was Tyler's friend.

We gave our approval (over Todd's slight objection), discussed a time for them to come home, and off they went—Todd with his "pesky" little brother, Tyler, following behind.

When they returned from their visit, they walked in the house chatting away, in seemingly good moods.

Everything about them seemed normal and positive. Then I noticed something out of the ordinary. Tyler's hair was wet and neatly combed as if he had just stepped out of the shower without time to dry it.

Both boys greeted Jan and me with a cheerful "hello" and headed to the kitchen for the evening feeding frenzy. I called them back and asked Tyler why his hair was wet. "Oh, that" he said, in as nonchalant a manner as he could muster. "I got a swirlie."

Now, I was an active boy as I grew up and got into my share of mischief. But I was unfamiliar with the term "swirlie." Neither of the boys seemed to want to talk about it—I just couldn't tell if it was because they knew I was not going to like it or because their bowls of ice cream were calling them from the kitchen.

I made them explain a "swirlie" to me. The boys said that to give someone a "swirlie," you pick them up by their feet, hold them upside down, and place their head in the toilet as it is flushed. The water swirling around in the toilet bowl also "swirls" around the person's head, drenching his hair—hence the name "swirlie."

The boys tried to convince me that "swirlies" are a normal part of youthful entertainment, that everyone's doing it, and that it is a boy's rite of passage into teenage coolness. After all, Tyler was going to be eleven years old soon; it was natural that the older guys at Kyle's house would give him a premature induction into "teen-hood."

Their fast-talking, positive spin didn't fool me. I did not believe it. It was an injustice to Tyler—*my son*—and I was *incensed*.

I asked Todd if he had participated in the prank, which immediately put him on the defense. He backpedaled, telling me he did not take part in it and assuring me that Tyler had been a problem the whole night. I said, "You stood off and let them do this to your brother!" Still on the defense, Todd said, "Dad, Tyler deserved it," as if this statement would get him off the hook and cinch my agreement with him.

Although I did not yell or become violent, I was noticeably upset. I turned and asked Tyler to follow me to the bedroom. When we were alone, I asked Tyler how he felt about what had been done to him. At first, he maintained the story, telling me everything was fine. Then I pointedly asked him, "Weren't you embarrassed?" He said nothing. "Are you frustrated ... upset? Do you feel violated?" I asked. Tears welled up in his eyes, and the truth came out. "Yeah, Dad," he said. "I was embarrassed, but they were bigger than me ...," his voice trailing off.

His response was all that was needed for me to take action. I marched into the living room and instructed Todd that as a brother, he was never to allow someone to violate one of his siblings in this type of degrading manner. It made no difference if Tyler was a pest and "deserved it." The commitment of the family requires us to defend each other in times of need. We cannot allow someone else to bring inappropriate correction or to violate one of our family members.

> *We cannot allow someone else to bring inappropriate correction or to violate one of our family members.*

I went on to say that the kind of love I expected among of our family was the kind of love I modeled for them—a protective love with respectful measures of correction. "I never want something like this to happen again," I told him. "Do you understand?" All Todd could muster was a timid, breathy, "Yes."

I then loaded Tyler into my car and drove to Kyle's house. I wanted to confront the boys responsible for the prank. I was controlled but firm. With carefully selected words, I told them that I did not approve of their behavior, and I asked them to apologize to Tyler. They did.

There were two things about this prank that brought about such a strong reaction in me. First, I cannot stand activity or behavior that gains enjoyment at someone else's expense. Second, I know if your family will not defend you, no one will.

This situation exposed two flaws in the attitudes of my boys. The first was a flaw in the way they found enjoyment. The second was a flaw in their commitment to family. My reaction to this situation let the boys know that their behavior was not consistent with my values for our family. Without my correction and modeling of the appropriate action, this situation would have sent a message of passive approval of their behavior. It would have deemed their actions as acceptable for family relationships and entertainment—a pattern that not only would be transferred to my children but also would ultimately be passed onto their own.

Avoiding Extremes

Over the years, I have observed several extremes in the ways parents respond to situations that impact their children. In order to take advantage of situations, using them for training and instruction, we must avoid these extremes as we walk with our children through their young lives.

THE OVER-NURTURING RESPONSE

The first extreme is a response of over-nurturing and over-protecting. This occurs when parents allow the love they have for their children to overpower their responsibility to train, prepare, and protect them. By coming to their children's defense or fighting their battles, parents shield their children from the lessons of life that are to be learned from trying circumstances.

Clayton Sr. was a tall, strong man with a deep, intimidating voice. Most of the neighborhood children stayed away from him when he was out in his yard. Clayton Jr. was big for his age and looked like he would follow his father's pattern for size. However, Clayton Jr. was a wimp. He was teased or picked on by nearly every child in the neighborhood. The teasing often became so mean-spirited that it brought Clayton Jr. to tears. This treatment of his son infuriated Clayton Sr., and when it happened, he would single out kids whom he felt had spearheaded the attack and yell at them. On several occasions, he marched over to the child's house and gave the parents of the offending child a very colorful piece of his mind.

However, his actions did not change the situation for his son. Rather than teach his son how to react to this type of adversity, Clayton Sr. came to his defense, fighting his battles for him. The result was a belief among the kids and many of the parents that Clayton Sr. was a grumpy, mean man. The response of his father increased disrespect for Clayton Jr. among his peers and produced an inability for him to stand up for himself in the face of teasing. He never learned how to stand and confront anything apart from his dad doing it for him.

Clayton Jr. and his family moved when he was in high school, but the situation did not change. His dad still fought his battles for him, perpetuating a weakness in adversity and a personality of insecurity. By fighting our children's battles for them, we produce weak and dependent children who lack the necessary skills for life and the ability to solve problems for themselves. Their weaknesses follow them right into adulthood where they face even more critical battles.

Parents should respond to their children's tough situations with loving care and sensitivity. This is positive and healthy. However, a caring parent should not shield his children from every unjust situation. *As a rule of thumb, I stepped in when a situation posed physical or emotional danger or when the age difference of those involved put my children at a disadvantage.* However, I was always careful not to involve myself in a way that obstructed the training benefit of the circumstance.

THE DETACHED RESPONSE

A second extreme is that of detachment. Detachment results when parents withdraw from personal intervention in their children's problems based on the belief that the children will fully benefit only when dealing with situations on their own. Detached parents fear the force of their personality might inappropriately determine a solution for their children. So, they withdraw from the circumstances to force their children to determine a solution on their own.

This detachment leaves children to deal with something for which they are not yet prepared. By contrast, children will grow in self-esteem and confidence as they respond to life's situations under the scrutiny of a caring parent.

A response of withdrawal is especially unproductive when the children have not reached the appropriate developmental level to be able to handle the situation. Children cannot be the judge of their own maturity level, so when they lack the relational or emotional development to know how to respond, a parent must step in to help them walk through the situation.

When Todd was four years old, our immediate neighbors both had boys his age. It was wonderful to have friends for our son to play with on the same side of the street within 100 feet of our front door. The three boys were good friends and playmates, but often they would fight over the same toy. Sometimes, two of the boys would join together to form an alliance against the other boy, and feelings or bodies would get hurt. The moms were usually the referees being called in to settle the disputes that arose among the boys.

One day Jan told me all the moms had decided not to referee any longer; instead, they would send the tattling boy back to the other two and make them work it out among themselves. It sounded like a good solution to me as it would force them to learn to solve their disputes and get along with each other. I agreed to support the decision if I was around when a dispute broke out.

All appeared to be working well the first few weeks after implementing the new strategy. The boys were still fighting, but they were forced to work it out, and the moms were less stressed by the tattling of the boys. One evening I walked in from work to the wailing of one of the boys as he stomped out of the bedroom area of our house. He was crying and screaming emphatically that he would never play with Todd again. As he stomped by me, I attempted to find out what had happened. My wife got my attention and reminded me that we had agreed not to involve ourselves in the boys' disputes. So, I let him go by me, crying and screaming out the front door on the way to his house. If the pattern held true, all would blow over by morning, and he would be back over to play. However, he did not come over the next day, and neither did the other boy.

When I arrived home from work the next night, Jan was mortified. One of the neighbors came down to tell us that Todd's friend had broken his collarbone in the scuffle the boys had over a plastic golf club the previous day. As they wrestled for control of the club, the boy lost the scuffle and fell into the doorknob. His crying departure the previous day was more than just a disagreement among the boys. When we learned what had happened, we immediately went to the parents and expressed our sorrow. We offered to pay their medical expenses. The parents were cool but polite and refused our offer. We asked if there was anything we could do, and they thanked us but said no.

Over the next couple days, the mothers of Todd's two friends got together and decided that Todd was mostly at fault and that he was more aggressive than their sons, posing a danger to their well-being. They decided not to let their sons play with Todd any longer. We tried everything we knew to make amends for the situation, but the parents were resolute in their conviction that Todd posed a danger to their boys.

Day after day Todd would watch as the two boys went from house to house, passing right by our driveway. As they went by Todd, they would chant, "We can't play with you. You're mean."

It broke our hearts to watch the disappointment on our son's face. His four-year-old mind did not understand why the boys would no longer play with him. Finally, having tried everything we could think of to resolve the issue, God opened a door for us to move.

As parents, we had removed ourselves too far from the situation, and the consequences were not good for the boys or us. It was the most emotionally and financially draining thing to impact our son and us in the early years of our family.

Parents must maintain open lines of communication with their children through all the stages of their development to know and understand the problems they're confronting. Each stage has unique challenges that must be overcome. When children are in the preschool years, it is easy to cut off communication due to their seemingly constant tattling on each other. However, to listen does not necessarily foster tattling as some may fear. Instead, it enables an evaluation of the situation and a determination of the children's ability to respond in an appropriate way. At this age, each situation requires some level of parental evaluation to determine the emotional and physical demands placed on the children, along with an assessment of the maturity level needed to respond properly. It is our responsibility to make sure our children are not out-manned physically or numerically as they respond to situations.

Parents must maintain open lines of communication with their children through all the stages of their development to know and understand the problems they're confronting.

Finally, we must monitor the outside factors working in the situation to make sure our children will not be overwhelmed. By outside factors, I mean things such as older children who may use their size or experience to take advantage or another parent who becomes involved in the situation. When one parent steps in, the other child's parents should become involved to provide balance and protection. Parental concerns must be addressed parent-to-parent to determine a helpful strategy that will benefit all involved in the situation.

By parental involvement and balance, I do not mean that another parent is forbidden from correcting my children without my permission. If my children are misbehaving and they are under the care of another adult, I want that adult to correct my children. However, when my children do not respond to the correction of that adult or when the behavior requires discipline beyond a time-out, I want to be involved.

THE CONTROLLING RESPONSE

This occurs when parents attempt to control the future or directional decisions of their children or the circumstances surrounding their children. They want to make sure everything is fair and right, shaded properly, and no one has an unfair advantage. Controlling parents use their wealth, social position, physical dominance, or authority to determine the outcome in situations involving their children.

In doing so, controlling parents create an artificial environment for their children, one that shields them from the consequences of their behavior or makes them dependent on the parents to direct their lives. Controlling parents see their responses as a protective shield, but this ultimately builds a defiant attitude of disrespect as children attempt to break free from their parents' control.

Eric and Judy are loving parents who have been involved in the activities of their children from preschool age and continue to be involved with their children who are now adults. When their middle child, Susan, graduated from college, they were there to celebrate. They helped her move to a new city to begin her career and were quite opinionated about she should live. They thought a gated apartment complex with on-site security was where she needed to live, but there were not many young singles who lived in the complex, and the rent was more than their daughter wanted to pay.

Susan knew of a different complex where she wanted to live. It was newly constructed and very popular with singles just beginning their careers. However, her parents insisted that she live in the complex they felt best and offered to pay the monthly difference so their daughter could live in safety. When Susan declined their offer, they were upset and used every conversation leading up to her move and even after she occupied her new apartment to restate their concerns. On one occasion Judy sent newspaper clippings of burglaries in the area and one in Susan's complex. They would not let the issue go away. Their attempt to control their daughter strained the relationship, and although she never completely rebelled against her parents' values, Susan did distance herself from them. Their relationship suffered as a result.

Another reaction children make to controlling parents is to comply with their control. It may look good from a distance, but this unhealthy dependence by children upon their parents actually weakens their ability to deal with people or issues, often turning children into relational "brats" who are unable to cope with any circumstance that does not conclude to their benefit.

Tim's parents controlled every aspect of his life. As a young, single adult, his parents had the final say on where he lived, the car he drove, and even whom he dated. Although Tim was living on his own and was several years into his work career, his parents dominated his life.

Tim made no decision without first discussing it with his parents and receiving their approval. He had learned that if he had their support in his decisions, then they would bail him out if he got in trouble. If he took action without their approval, he was on his own.

Tim struggled with making and keeping friends and finding a girlfriend who would put up with the control his parents exerted in his life. As a result, he was lonely and very underdeveloped in his social skills. Tim's dependence upon his parents stunted his growth as an adult and made him unable to stand on his own. Rather than providing encouragement and counsel to help him while still allowing him to make his own decisions, his parents controlled his life in an unhealthy way.

These extremes keep our children from developing into stable, balanced adults. Let me explain the difference between correction and control. When I observe behavior in my children that is inconsistent with my standard of values, I correct their behavior. I expect a change, and if I do not see a change, discipline is initiated. *Correction is a response to the child and his behavior. Control is an attempt to manipulate the circumstances and the people involved toward a determined outcome.* When children are young and while they live in at home, it is appropriate to exert some control over their lives. But we must be careful even then not to build a pattern of dependent control between our children and ourselves.

When our children leave home to establish lives of their own, we must assume the role of advisor. Our good intentions or concerns for our children do not justify any attempt to control them or the circumstances of their life. Controlling responses instill weakness in our children. They also erect barriers of resistance that can damage and even destroy the relationship we have with them.

Our good intentions or concerns for our children do not justify any attempt to control them or the circumstances of their life.

The goal of good parenting is to avoid extremes in responses and to find a balance that protects children as they deal with circumstances but also allows them to gain experience and training in preparation for life. We must protect our children from unfair situations while extracting from the circumstances their fullest instructional value.

Parents must learn when to lend assistance to their children, when to come to their defense, when to support them, and when to allow them to stand up and fight for themselves. We must learn when and how to use circumstances for their highest instructional purpose. Finding balance in situations affecting our children takes proactive effort and diligent sensitivity to ensure we do not lose the instructive benefits of the situations. Our children need to learn how to extract benefit from every circumstance before they leave home. They will use this important skill throughout their adult lives.

A Concluding Thought

Jesus taught and modeled the principle of transference to His disciples. He told them that students are not above their teacher, and the students will learn what the teacher has experienced. Do you see God in the circumstances of your life? Is He recognized and included in the situations that arise in your business, pleasure, and family?

It is critical to develop an awareness of God's involvement in life's circumstances so you can gain an understanding on how to partner with Him as He works. An awareness of God's work and your partnership with Him will maximize the learning benefit in every situation.

Section Three

Supporting Standards

The Importance of Spending Time with Your Children

Special memories enjoyed with our children are the result of accumulated times of mundane activities, committed work, and patient efforts to build understanding and communication.

T he average father spends less than five minutes each day with his children.

When I first heard this statistic, I dismissed it as absurd. I thought of all our family activities and how often I involved myself in the lives of my children. I concluded the report must be in error. However, as I have interacted with other men, I have become convinced the statement is true, at least as it relates to the quality of time fathers give to their children. I have become aware that the majority of the time fathers spend with their children is not quality time. Like the saying, "The lights are on, but no one is home," it seems when fathers are with their children, they are present in body but distracted by thoughts of work or other concerns. Their lights are on, but no one is home!

I believe there are two major reasons men are distracted and disconnected from their children. First, men usually work in an ordered environment, subject to time schedules and deadlines. The home environment is often just the opposite—chaotic and disjointed. Children are naturally active and bring a certain amount of disorder to the home. This sense of chaos is compounded if the children are undisciplined, loud, demanding, selfish, or out of control, which all children are to some degree. Children naturally behave this way; it is part of their foolish nature, and it changes very little as they mature into their teen years.

If children are not trained, their undisciplined and out of control behavior will follow them right into adulthood. Proactive parenting, the kind that is involved and focused, is needed to train children how to act.

The chaotic and disjointed atmosphere that often surrounds children can lead a father to detach himself emotionally when they are young. Once he has disconnected, he will most often remain this way through every stage of their development.

The second reason men's attentions are turned away from their children is due to the demands placed on them by their careers or their involvement in a wide variety of personal interests. Men often find it difficult to balance family time with a full slate of work responsibilities and the demands of friends, hobbies, civic clubs, and other similar interests. After working hard, it is easy for a man to justify a selfish focus centered on his needs and to reward himself with activities that offer personal gratification and excitement. With this type of competition for undivided attention, it is easy to understand—*although it doesn't make it right*—why men end up distracted and unfocused toward their children, spending their free time other places. Children are the most demanding and least gratifying of their choices.

We often make shortsighted decisions because it is difficult for us to consider the long-term benefits of sacrificial investment in the lives of our children. We perpetuate our insensitivity with the deceptive thought that we can make it all work, not recognizing we have given the best of our time and emotions somewhere else—leaving us with nothing to give to our children. Deep down we know we cannot do it all, but it is difficult to make the tough decisions that put priorities in the right place. The price we pay is missed opportunities to train and influence our children.

Using the Opportunity of Time

Most men savor great moments in sports. What man would not have wanted to be present to watch Joe Frazier upset Mohammad Ali for the heavyweight boxing title? Or to see the American hockey team beat the Russians in the Olympics for the gold medal? Great moments—the ones remembered with meaning—are best enjoyed when they are experienced firsthand. Highlights and reruns do not compare. To fully experience the thrill of the event, one must be there when it happens. It's as simple as that.

If we could predict a great moment, we could arrange our schedules so that we could be there to experience it firsthand. However, this is often not possible. Instead, it takes sacrifice, priority, and commitment to create opportunities that make it possible to witness great moments. This is true with sporting events as well as great moments with our children. A father's presence is a catalyst for producing great moments, ones that develop meaningful memories with his children.

> *It takes sacrifice, priority,*
> *and commitment to create*
> *opportunities that make it possible*
> *to witness great moments.*

Absentee and distracted fathers miss the greatest moments of their children's lives, only experiencing them in "highlights" or "reruns." I remember watching my son score the winning goal for his soccer team, meeting my daughter's first date, watching my children learn to swim, helping them with their homework, and witnessing a thousand other significant events in their lives. *I have never regretted sacrificing the time.*

As my children have grown to be adults, my perspective of their childhood has changed. I realized too slowly the shortness of their time in our home. When they were young, their college years and beyond seemed an eternity away. The year our oldest son (Todd) graduated from high school was the first time it hit me. I saw how quickly he had grown up, and I regretted not spending more quality time with him. There was so much more I wanted to share with him to be sure he was prepared for adult responsibilities and opportunities. There was so much more I wanted to teach him. It seemed as though I blinked my eyes, and he was headed off to college.

I determined right then and there to make a change to ensure I did not repeat this mistake with our remaining children. I also went back and invested in Todd's life in a greater way.

I sat down one morning to write out the subjects I wished I had covered with Todd more completely. I quickly came up with a dozen subjects I wanted to cover and explain in greater depth to make sure he had a solid basis of understanding for things he would encounter as an adult.

These subjects included the most essential quality to look for in a wife, the most important principle in financial management, and what really makes a person successful. These were subjects we had talked about many times, but I was insecure in the thoroughness of my training.

I decided I would write Todd a weekly email and present to him my thoughts and perspective on these important subjects. Through the beauty of email communication, he could print off my thoughts for consideration at a convenient time and then respond back to me with his comments or questions.

I felt this was the second-best thing next to face-to-face communication. I borrowed the format from Josh McDowell, the Campus Crusade for Christ leader, teacher, and author. He actually wrote love letters to his son and daughter while they were in college. His letters became the text for two of his books. The format was loving and interactive rather than stuffy and preachy. Before I started sending my emails, I told Todd what I was going to do and why. He happily received my input because he knew my motive was love for him.

I also decided to establish personal times with each of our other three children to give greater opportunities for memorable moments. One way I accomplished this was to treat each of my children to breakfast or lunch regularly. I began having a weekly lunch with Lisa, our oldest daughter and second child, during her senior year of high school. We had a time each week for just the two of us to be together. There was no specific agenda. We would simply talk about whatever might come up in the conversation, express feelings or thoughts from the day, or talk about an event from the morning or one coming later in the day. When Tyler, our third child, became a senior, I continued the weekly lunch with him. These lunches produced special memories with both Lisa and Tyler.

I decided not to wait until the senior year of our youngest child, Lindsay, to share one-on-one time with her. We ate breakfast together at least once a week. I got the full load of joy, concerns, and information from our most expressive child. These times with my children produced great moments, priceless memories worth more than great riches. The special times we shared will be relived and enjoyed over and over in the years ahead.

In addition, I have sought to communicate to my children that they always have priority in my life—at home and at work. My assistant knows I am always available to my children by telephone and in person. My instructions are if my children need me, I am to be interrupted. When my children visit or call me at work, I am not concerned about my pressing responsibilities or my children's insensitivity to my business. Rather, I am concerned that I communicate at all times my love and care for them. I have taught them to be respectful of people and my schedule while demonstrating to them in real terms that they come first.

This concept did not originate with me but with my heavenly Father. It is how He responds to me. He is always available to listen to my concerns, comfort my emotions, and provide for my needs. He is never too busy for me. To teach my children to understand God's love and care, I must mirror God's actions to the best of my ability.

> *To teach my children to understand*
> *God's love and care, I must mirror*
> *God's actions to the best of my ability.*

My dad showed me the way. During my last semester of college before graduation, I was in the process of interviewing for a job. One evening Jan and I went over to my parents' house for dinner. As my dad and I sat in the den talking and waiting to be called to the table, he reached into his pocket and handed me his business card. On the back, he had written this brief message: *I am your best friend, and I will always be your best friend. If you ever need me, call, no matter when, where, or what time it is ... Love, Dad.*

This was the most important gift I received for my college graduation, though in a monetary sense, it was the least expensive. In fact, it is the only gift I received that I can still remember today. I carried that card in my billfold until several years after my dad passed away. Occasionally I would take it out and re-read the message. What a gift from my dad!

I have found you can never recapture the important opportunity created by a crisis of concern, an emotional trauma, or a pressing need. A kind word, a gentle touch, or a solution to a critical problem at the moment of need creates impressions in our children's minds they will never forget.

Developing a Long-Term Perspective

Today the virtues of self-sacrifice and delayed gratification are not widely taught or embraced. Most of us have been persuaded to think only about ourselves and only for the moment. We do not want to wait until tomorrow, next week, next month, or next year. If we want something, we want it *now*. As these two important virtues have slipped away from our culture, they have taken with them an appreciation for the value of our time. Our time has value, and we should invest it with thoughtful consideration to achieve the maximum return.

Our time has value, and we should invest it with thoughtful consideration to achieve the maximum return.

To produce a great return on the investment we make in our children, it helps to think in financial terms. The value of our time can easily be converted into a dollar value so that the investment we make can be evaluated like any other financial opportunity. For example, consider a man with an annual income of $36,000. If he works five days a week, 40-hours a week, with two weeks of vacation a year, he will work 2,000 hours during the calendar year. By dividing the hours into his salary, his annual income is converted into a value of $18 per hour. We can now use this hourly rate to convert a favorite activity into its cost in time. For example, a round of golf that takes four hours of time converts into a cost of $72, on top of green fees. A new bass or ski boat used every weekend might convert into a half-year or more of time dollars on top of the purchase price and operating cost of the boat itself.

When we include in our thinking the cost of our time, along with the cost of the purchase, we become aware of the total costs associated with the item we desire. The physical and mental costs associated with our work have a clearly defined dollar value. Following this process more often as we evaluate the need and timing of a purchase would help us properly prioritize it by considering the investment of our time.

Spending time with our children should be viewed as any investment for the future. For example, many employees participate in a retirement plan in which they can invest a certain amount of money each pay period. The theory is that a small amount regularly invested over a long period of time can accumulate into a large amount through the miracle of compound interest. When preparing for retirement, it is wisest to begin early in life and invest small amounts that will have a long time to grow, rather than waiting until you can invest a large amount that will not have the benefit of compounding interest.

Similarly, if you begin when your children are young and invest consistent amounts of time (even if the amounts are not as large as you would like), your investment in your children will compound into a tremendous treasure. The amount you invest may seem insignificant today, but it will compound to produce a great return.

I know a man who is by almost every measure a man of great success. He has overcome obstacles to become a huge success in his career. Through his business success, he has achieved great financial wealth as well. He has paid a great price for his success, though: he is never home or available for his children. Now, he has provided them with a comfortable lifestyle, and there is no doubt he loves his children. However, he has missed most of their big events. He has not been there to see their athletic victories, their awards banquets, or their recitals.

This pattern started when his children were young and continued into their adult lives. When his oldest son got caught with drugs in his car, the man was not there to deal with the situation because he was on a business trip. When another son was honored at his company's annual awards banquet by being inducted into The President's Council of Young Leaders, he wasn't there. Even though he was notified beforehand of his son's award, he could not (or did not) rearrange his schedule to be there to share in this important event in his son's life.

I don't know the thinking of this father. Perhaps he was detached and insensitive to the opportunities he missed. Maybe he was acting toward his children just like his dad had responded to him. Maybe he thought he could wait until a better time, comforting himself with the false idea that at some future moment he could make up for his absence. Unfortunately, this moment often never comes, or if it does, his children will have built lives that have no room for sharing important moments with him.

Regardless of his thinking, this I know—every father, even very busy ones, must invest time in small increments, at important moments, and in mundane circumstances. He must declare through his actions that his children are an important priority in his life. It cannot be put off until a better time because there may not be one.

The Benefits of an Investment Strategy

Over the years, I have invested time in my children. I have memories of wonderful events, and today I am enjoying the benefits of my investment strategy.

Let me share a return that I received on the investment I made in my oldest son. My life is rich with examples like this from each of my children, the result of compound interest that has accrued on the investment I have made of my time.

On December 30, 1995, Todd married a wonderful young woman. Days before the wedding, we celebrated Christmas with our daughter-in-law-to-be for the first time. It was an exciting and emotional celebration, a time of significant change in our family. When the time arrived for me to open my gift from Todd, he presented me with a package about the size of a shirt box. I shook it and could not imagine what it could be. It was much heavier than a shirt.

I tore away the wrapping paper and discovered a picture frame. Mounted in the frame was a poem, neatly printed and matted.

Todd said he had written the poem for me as he thought about the step he was taking into marriage. He said I had taught him so many things, things he wanted to pass onto his children, and he wanted to express his appreciation with words. I could not contain my emotions as I read. I want to share his poem with you:

Lessons of a Father

To learn how to fly with a gentle nudge,
To learn to forgive and not hold a grudge.
To know how to talk with a bridled tongue,
To know how to walk and lead the young.
To follow the advice and counsel of peers,
To follow God's Word will enhance your years.
To give with a heart that feels better when done,
To give with the love of God for His Son.
To know it's all right for a man to cry,
To know it will hurt when we say good-bye.
To love and live an enjoyable life,
To love my family and honor my wife.
To see the good in a ridiculous mess,
To see that my children have a place to rest.
To never give reason to question your word,
To never let anger from your mouth be heard.
To learn to encourage with a simple smile,
To learn that the best go the extra mile.
I pattern my life after the lessons I've learned,

The teaching goes on, but now it's my turn.
I go with strength from the training I've had,
These are the things I've learned from my dad

—Todd Lane

A Concluding Thought

I can truthfully say that the time Jan and I have invested in each of our four children has been the best investment we ever made—the most rewarding and the most profitable. It has returned to us far more than we could have ever imagined!

How are you investing your time? Are you prioritizing a portion of your time for your children? Or are you waiting for the day when you can make a big deposit of time and missing the compounding benefits of a little invested on a regular basis?

I once heard this description of what it is like to work for the telephone company: some days you dig holes, some days you plant poles, some days you string wire, and some days you make a connection. Without the holes, poles, and wire, there will not be a connection. Special memories enjoyed with our children are the result of consistent times of mundane activities, committed work, and patient efforts to build understanding and communication. What great joy there is when it all comes together in a finished product.

It is not too late for you to dig holes, plant poles, and string wire. It's not too late to make investment deposits in your children's lives. Your children may even be adults now, perhaps with children of their own. Don't worry; there is still time. Your effort and the investment of your time will bring awesome rewards.

12

The Balance of Two Perspectives

My wife increases my effectiveness as a father.
Her support, insight, and perspective minimize
my weaknesses and compound my strengths.

K ing Solomon, possibly the richest king and
certainly considered to be one of the wisest men
in the history of the world, made a simple yet profound
statement: "Two are better than one ... For if they fall,
one will lift up his companion" (Ecclesiastes 4:9–10).

This statement is true in business relationships as well
as in marriage. My wife increases my effectiveness as a
father. Her support, insight, and perspective minimize
my weaknesses and compound my strengths. We are
partners working together to rear our children.

As I have counseled engaged, newlywed, and married
couples over the years, I have been struck by the way
God designed the mechanism of attraction between a
man and a woman. The relationship often begins with
physical attraction, only to continue if both people

have common life goals, dreams, and interests. Once this important foundation is in place, there is diversity in just about every other facet of their lives. A quiet person tends to attract an outgoing and gregarious one. A high-strung, opinionated person attracts an easy-going, "whatever" type, and so on.

My wife, Jan, and I are this way. She is fun-loving, spontaneous, and talkative. I tend to be more organized, less spontaneous, and more introspective. Together, we share a common intensity related to our commitment to God. We passionately desire to love and serve Him. In most other ways, Jan and I are different from each other.

I write this as encouragement for you so that you will embrace and respect the differences in your wife. As a good friend of mine says, "If you're both the same, one of you is unnecessary."

These differences are what attracted you to your spouse in the first place. I am embarrassed to admit that for too many years of my marriage, my constant effort was to mold my wife into my image. When we disagreed, I would try to help her get the "right" perspective. I "knew" my way was always better than hers, and I was confident it was the "right" way to respond. I rarely, if ever, gave Jan credit for having a beneficial perspective unless it lined up with mine. When children arrived in our home, parenting revealed new differences in our perspectives.

Who is right? Is one way better than another? The male ego wants to dictate the response to circumstances and in doing so works against any perspective not its own. But in reality, a variety of experiences produce a perspective that brings new insights and options to any situation.

Rather than try to change your wife into your likeness, seek to understand her and embrace her uniqueness by accepting and celebrating the way she is different from you. By doing so, you will allow her perspective to minimize your weaknesses and add to your strengths.

> *Seek to understand her and embrace her uniqueness by accepting and celebrating the way she is different from you.*

Differences Add Strength

As Jan and I came to embrace each other's differences, we realized a great advantage in our parenting. Our children knew if they wanted cake, candy, or pop between meals, they had better ask me, not their mom. If they wanted compassion for forgetting a responsibility, they knew to go to their mom, not me.

How do our children figure these things out? They are not concerned with ego, authority structure, or roles of responsibility; our children are simply attempting to get what they want! Over time, they learn the easiest and most successful ways. When parents become occupied with trying to change each other, they find themselves in constant competition and miss bringing the power and strength of unity into their relationship.

As you honestly examine your personality and its influence on your behavior, you will be able to admit your weaknesses and lean on your partner's strength. Even if your wife is not strong in your area of weakness, you can maximize results by trusting that two heads are better than one. A unified decision will always accomplish more than a decision based on individual perspective.

> *A unified decision will always*
> *accomplish more than a decision based*
> *on individual perspective.*

Keys to Unified Decisions

Never be pressured into a decision. As a parent, always keep in mind that you are in charge. You do not have to make decisions under pressure.

Children apply pressure to get the decision they want. They often present an issue with unrealistic time constraints. They ask for an immediate decision—"This is a once-in-a-lifetime opportunity! We have to decide right now!" Our rule of thumb for pressure situations in which time did not allow full consideration of the details was to say "no." Some requests can be decided upon quickly; others need careful consideration and discussion.

Children need to learn patience and gain an understanding that God's plan will succeed regardless of timeframe or circumstances. Making hurried decisions is one of the best ways to miss God's plan. If the opportunity is right, careful consideration and discussion will produce the response they desire and confirm God's hand in the process. If some good opportunities are missed in the process, it will not be the end of the world. More bad opportunities will be avoided than good ones missed.

Never undermine your partner. All children are born with an innate ability to manipulate. When children do not receive the response they want from one parent, they will often attempt an "end-run" appeal with the other parent. An "end-run" usually involves some deceit on our children's part because they fail to disclose the already communicated decision while repeating their request to the parent being manipulated.

On those few occasions in which they do reveal the decision made by the other parent, it is to benefit their appeal of the decision as seeming unfair, lacking understanding of the circumstances, or being totally uncompassionate! Regardless of the method, children can argue pretty convincingly, sometimes generating anger and judgment toward our spouse. Be careful of this attempt to divide and conquer!

Jan and I responded to situations like these by supporting each other's decisions, even if we disagreed. If either of us felt a decision was in error, we discussed it behind closed doors without our children's knowledge. If we needed to make a change, the one who originally made the decision communicated the change to the children, along with the reasons for the change.

Use each other's strengths to make the best decisions as a team. If we allow pride or ego to stand in the way of our ability to join our strengths and cover our weaknesses, we miss the opportunity to arrive at the best solution. A husband and wife must lean on each other, even deferring to one another in the decision-making process.

> *If we allow pride or ego to stand in the way of our ability to join our strengths and cover our weaknesses, we miss the opportunity to arrive at the best solution.*

When Todd entered junior high, he came home one day excited about a school dance scheduled for the coming weekend. He wanted to go and could hardly wait.

Jan was dead set against him going. Because she is more outgoing and party-loving than I am, she had better insight into the pressures and temptations Todd would encounter during and after the dance with his friends. She thought he was too young to be exposed to those pressures and temptations.

I felt Todd should be allowed to go with clearly defined parameters. The dance would provide a good training vehicle for our maturing son. Jan had strong reservations, but she listened to my position, and we worked together to reach a decision we both could accept. Together we created a safe and fun experience for Todd, one that allowed us to watch and participate. We agreed to be parent chaperones. Our son got to experience the dance, and we got to monitor his experience.

Maintaining Unity After Divorce

If you are divorced, put aside personal disagreements with your ex-spouse and work together for the benefit of your children. Over half of all marriages are now dissolved through divorce, and most of those marriages have produced children.

Divorce often has a negative impact on a man's interest and ability to remain involved with his children. If you are a divorced parent, you must set aside the animosity and hurt associated with your relationship and continue to balance your perspectives through a parenting partnership for the blessing and benefit of your children. You can still create a heritage for them, even if it didn't work in your marriage.

To do this, you must communicate with each other about any issues of concern related to the children. Also, *you must agree to support each other's authority during conversations with your children.* When you disagree with each other, do so privately, away from the children, in a place where you will not be overheard.

If you or your ex-spouse have remarried, do not allow disagreement or conflict with the new spouse to enter into your parenting partnership. You and your ex-spouse are the parents, but through remarriage, secondary partners have been introduced into the parenting process. Agree to work with your ex-spouse's new partner to benefit the children.

Children rarely, if ever, want their parents to separate or divorce. If you are divorced, I urge you to make a commitment to set aside unresolved issues for the benefit of your children, no matter how overwhelming the task may seem. Working together, you can bring security and blessing to your children even though it is too late to restore your marriage.

A Concluding Thought

I have related many of my experiences as a father in the chapters of this book. However, it was not my influence alone that produced great children. My influence on my children would have been less effective without the partnership of my wife. As I conclude this chapter, I leave you with some questions to consider:

Have you expressed your appreciation to your wife for the contribution she has made to your children's development and your parental success? Have you fully appreciated the unique qualities and individual strengths your wife contributes to your marriage and family?

Take a minute to thank God for the gift He has given to you in the person of your wife. Then be sure to follow that prayer of thanksgiving with a verbal expression of thanks to her. Why not make renewed commitments to capitalize on each other's strengths as you parent your children? A decision to do this will greatly enhance your influence as a father.

13

Preparing Children for Their Destiny

*To find their destiny, children cannot be left to self-develop
or shoved into the same mold as each other, or a mold that
parents determine is best for them, without consideration
of God's plan for their lives.*

T hose who desire to fulfill their purpose in life must
begin with the belief that there is a reason for
which they were created.

To even approach this thought, we must understand
that life is not the result of a cosmic accident. Rather,
we must believe that God is the sovereign Creator
and sustainer of all things, animate and inanimate. If
God is the Creator and sustainer of our intricate and
amazing universe, then logic tells us He must be doing
it for a purpose. He must also have a divine plan for
each of His creatures to fit into—a destiny they were
born to fulfill.

The Bible confirms this argument when it reveals
God knew us before our conception and was involved

in the gestational development of our physical form in our mothers' wombs (Jeremiah 1:5). It further declares God has plans for us that are good and not evil, and these plans give us hope for the future (Jeremiah 29:11).

One of my greatest desires has been to help my children understand how God has created them for a purpose. It is an awesome responsibility to work with them to discover what their unique purpose is. I am not a psychologist, but I know in real terms that my children's self-concept—their understanding of who they are—and their positive feelings about themselves are directly linked to their understanding of the God-ordained purpose for their lives. *Their ability to be content in life's circumstances comes from recognizing that in order to fulfill His plan, God has purpose and involvement in each situation they encounter.*

I must be careful to see my children as God sees them and relate to them with the understanding that they have purpose defined from the heart of God. If I treat my children like intrusions in my life or unnecessary interruptions in my schedule, rather than precious gifts from God; if I act like they lack value or potential instead of reinforcing their importance to God; if I berate them and belittle them when they make mistakes, rather than correcting and instructing them in the proper methods and desired results—then my methods and influence will not help them understand their unique purpose or lead them to achieve their destiny.

I must be careful to see my children
as God sees them and relate to them
with the understanding that they have
purpose defined from the heart of God.

The influence of a father is not to be used to predetermine or mold his children into what he wants them to be. Instead, he is to use his influence in their lives to help them discover their God-given destiny by developing and nurturing their strengths, desires, interests, and abilities, and then encouraging them to go for it!

Discovering Purpose

I was in my early teens the first time I remember seriously considering what I was going to do with my life. I knew I wanted to marry and have a career like my dad. I wanted to be successful and influential like him. Pure and simple, I wanted to be like my dad!

When I graduated from college, I began to interview for employment. I talked to my dad's business partners about working for their company. "You know, Tom," my dad kept reassuring me, "you do not have to do what I am doing."

My dad thoroughly enjoyed his work and his career, working for the same company for over 40 years. He started by filling orders in the warehouse, and he finished his career with the same company as a principal owner. He loved his work, but he also understood I might not love it as much as he did. He did not want me to follow him into his business just to please him; he wanted me to find peace, happiness, and fulfillment as he had. These qualities are achieved through knowing and fulfilling God's purpose.

As I sought to guide my children in their search for purpose, I kept two things in mind. First, I knew God designed each of my children for a unique purpose. *God's plan for me may not be (and probably won't be) His plan for them.* As their father, I was not to determine or legislate for them my predetermined ideas for their lives. Instead, my place was to help them find God's unique purpose for their lives. Which brings me to my second thought: How could I help my children do this? How could I best guide them without placing my own expectations and ambitions on them?

Guiding Children on the Road to Destiny

Many parents mistakenly think they will send their eighteen-year-old sons and daughters off to college to "figure out" what they want to do with their lives. These college experiences may launch them into careers but not necessarily into their destiny. The groundwork for destiny must be laid far before college.

When Todd was months away from his fourteenth birthday, Jan and I learned about a summer mission program from a friend who was in town to minister at our church. He told us his grandchildren had participated in it and how it had blessed and revolutionized their lives. As we discussed the mission organization and its thrust to provide teenagers with worldwide mission opportunities, Jan and I thought this type of experience might be good for Todd.

We realized Todd was entering the years when he would make decisions that would determine his future, so we felt prompted to challenge him with a bigger view of the world. Todd was about to finish the eighth grade; he was looking with anticipation toward the move into high school that would come in the fall. But we were concerned that his high school experience would not encourage him to ask questions related to his purpose or pose solutions that would be larger than the United States. We knew God was bigger than the United States. His Kingdom is all over the world, and the universe is His dwelling place. So, we approached Todd with two options: he could work on one of 50 different summer mission projects with the worldwide mission organization our friend told us about, or he could attend a Christian high school in the fall.

Unenthused about either option, Todd was particularly reluctant about the mission trip; it would mean giving up his whole summer before high school. Nevertheless, we wanted him to think globally for opportunities in his life and gain an experiential understanding and vision for life that was bigger than our town, state, or nation. Because the world is God's kingdom, His work is worldwide. We wanted Todd to have this perspective as he considered his future and God's specific purpose for his life. We wanted him to view the whole world as a possibility.

We had several discussions about Todd's decision. The mission trip was expensive, costing about $2,800. The mission organization strongly encouraged the trip expense to be raised through donations from family and friends, rather than paid by the parents. Todd, Jan, and I arrived at this agreement: we would select a specific mission service project and submit the paperwork. In the meantime, we prayed if it was not God's will for Todd to go, he would not be accepted, or the funds would not be contributed.

A few weeks later, Todd was accepted, and the financial support was raised from family and friends. God's will had been revealed and confirmed in his life. Todd spent the summer before high school in Ireland, building a recreation center at a Christian retreat facility. More significant than his work on the project, though, was his newly developed awareness of God's work on a global scale.

Years later when Todd graduated from college with a degree in finance, he went to work for an international corporation. His employment began in the United States, but as I mentioned in Chapter 9, advancement opportunities took him and his wife to live in New Zealand. They lived in Auckland on assignment for his company and became involved in a vibrant, growing church, surrounded by many caring Christian friends. Their adjustment to a new country and culture, their success in finding a place of service, and their ability to build friendships were the results of the foundation developed through experiences like the summer mission project.

To find God's purpose, we must be willing to obey and follow Him—wherever He may lead. Business success is wonderful and brings financial rewards and freedom. But without an understanding of the higher purpose and call of God, financial rewards and freedom are mere tokens of an economic system that provides no eternal value or purpose. The things that last are those which we do out of an obedient heart for God and His Kingdom, things that fulfill God's divine plan for our lives. There is nothing more satisfying.

To find God's purpose, we must be
willing to obey and follow Him—
wherever He may lead.

No Cookie-Cutter Molds

All of my children are now adults with spouses and children of their own. Todd is the only one who participated in a summer mission project. I say this to emphasize that the issue is not to send your children on a summer mission project, as good as that may be. The issue is to explore the uniqueness of God's plan for each child He entrusts to your care.

All of my children are different. They have unique personalities, abilities, talents, and interests. To find their destiny, children cannot be left to self-develop or shoved into the same mold as each other, or a mold that parents determine is best for them, without consideration of God's plan for their lives.

As parents, we must develop our children's desire to seek, find, and fulfill God's plan for their lives. Then with guidance and oversight, we must allow our children to explore opportunities with the confidence that God will lead them to fulfill His purpose.

Parents often thwart their children's discovery of purpose due to legitimate concerns that are not handled properly. Discovery of purpose is a process in our children that can be confused with instability if not correctly evaluated. Some parents have dreams for their children's future, living out their own unfulfilled desires through the children's lives. These parents do not support the discovery process unless it conforms to the dreams they have for their children. God intends parents to guide children in their discovery of *His* purpose and plan through the parent-child relationship, but in this scenario, a tug-of-war begins. The parents push their personal desires on the children, and the children resist, causing frustration and missed opportunities for both parties.

Three Steps to Destiny

What can you do to help your children discover and fulfill their destiny? Here are three guidelines to follow:

TEACH YOUR CHILDREN THAT GOD IS THEIR CREATOR AND HE HAS A PLAN AND A PURPOSE FOR THEIR LIVES.

Encourage your children in the discovery of their strengths, abilities, and interests. As you do this, your children will develop a proper perspective for the times when they fail—at a job, project, relationship, or commitment. Every person fails at some point; it is a natural part of life. Failing doesn't make them a failure; quitting does.

You and I have learned from our mistakes. Our children will learn from theirs. It is our role as parents to help them understand what went wrong and identify the characteristics that might be useful in understanding God's plan for their lives. We must do this without condemning or shaming them for not succeeding.

ALLOW DIVERSITY TO BE A PART OF THE DISCOVERY PROCESS.

I have a brother-in-law whose discovery of purpose developed through a different process than mine. However, he found a place of productivity and influence. In the early years of his adult life, he seemed unstable because he skipped from job to job in what seemed to be a whimsical approach to life. He appeared flighty and unfocused compared to the other men in our family, including myself, who had discovered the purpose and direction God had for their lives more quickly and without trying different jobs.

Although it took my brother-in-law a little more time, he found and defined his purpose. My point is that not everyone will follow the same path to find God's plan for their life, but everyone who desires to serve and obey God will be directed by Him as they seek to discover and fulfill His purpose.

Everyone who desires to serve
and obey God will be directed
by Him as they seek to discover
and fulfill His purpose

GIVE PRIORITY ATTENTION TO ISSUES
OF CHARACTER IN YOUR CHILDREN.

Every parent must realize that there are tests to be passed on the road to fulfilling one's destiny. To test the strength of our children's character, God determines and allows circumstances to occur in their lives. He will not move our children forward until they pass the grade level tests He sends their way. God's work in the process of their development will not excuse their character defects; therefore, we do our children no favors when we excuse them.

When you see laziness, slothfulness, disloyalty, rebellion, or other character flaws in your children, you must be diligent in addressing them. The younger your children are when you begin this process, the better. As your children grow into their upper teen years, the clay of their lives begins to harden and is no longer easily molded. Eventually, it becomes so hard that any change must be chiseled—sometimes pretty forcefully—in order to bring conformity with God's purpose. *Failure to give attention to issues of character is one reason that our children seem to get stuck in a repeating pattern of destructive failure.* Their faulty character negatively influences their behavior and keeps them from discovering the fullness of God's purpose for their lives.

A Concluding Thought

Francis of Assisi wrote, "Keep a clear eye toward life's end. Do not forget your purpose and destiny as God's creature. What you are in His sight is what you are and nothing more."

How about you? Have you been aware of God's purpose and destiny for your life? Have you sought to raise your children with an understanding that God created them and He has a plan for their lives? Have you seen something in the context of this chapter that you need to change in the way you relate to your children? If you will acknowledge your failure and ask for God's help, He will put your parenting influence back on the right track. Why not do it right now? As you turn to God today, He will give you the wisdom and ability to participate with your children in the discovery of their divine destiny!

14

Raising Righteous Teenagers

The rod and rebuke give wisdom,
But a child left to himself brings shame to his mother
(Proverbs 29:15).

I spent most of my teenage years looking ahead to the next season of my life and resenting people who looked down on my age. I felt I was more mature and capable of handling more responsibility than most adults gave me credit. Talk to almost any teenager, and you will find some version of these feelings being played out in his or her life.

By definition, a teenager is a person between the ages of thirteen and nineteen years. These years are an awkward stage of development between childhood and adulthood and present some very interesting challenges to the parenting process. When relating to a teenager, sometimes we don't know which person to relate to—the child we know or the adult beginning to emerge.

Consider the paradoxes represented in these statements and see if you can recognize your teenager in them:

A teenager is a person who can't remember to take out the trash but never forgets a phone number. A teenager "diets" by giving up candy bars before breakfast. A teenager is someone who can hear a song by his favorite artist played three blocks away but can't hear his mother calling from the next room. A teenager can operate the latest computer, video game, or electronic gadget without a lesson but can't remember to make his bed or take out the trash. A teenager has the time and energy to chat online for hours or talk on the phone past midnight but doesn't have the strength to help with chores around the house. A teenager struggles to make it to dinner, work, or class on time but isn't a minute late for a rock concert or a date. A teenager is a person who believes his thoughts are original and innovative but can't imagine his parents as younger than thirty!

The teenage years bring unique challenges and opportunities, as does each stage of development. Parents of young children are in complete control of their children's lives, directing every aspect, imparting values, and encouraging proper actions. As children grow toward adulthood, parenting becomes less about directing and more about advising. A parent ultimately occupies the role of advisor or mentor in his adult child's life.

During each stage of your children's development, your responsibility is to guide them along the path of life, imparting values, developing and defining talents, and creating a self-concept based on a present awareness of God and His love. In the years leading to adulthood, the process of parenting enters a new and critical stage. The teenage years are the final stage of self-discovery that determines whether your son or daughter becomes an adult prepared to fulfill God's purpose independent from your direct control, though not apart from your guiding influence.

3 Things Every Teenager Needs

There are three things your teenager needs more than ever during this stage of his life.

Your teenager needs to know how much you care about him. Communicating to him that you understand the demands and pressures he faces is critical for success. However, simply knowing you care is not enough. This knowledge must be linked with an understanding of his feelings. When this happens, it communicates empathy for what he is experiencing and establishes a bond between the two of you.

Your teenager needs to know the "why" and "how" of what you believe. Often, he will need to debate and test it to know exactly how it works for you and to see how to make it work for his life. Forcing your teenager to adopt your values through legalistic enforcement is a guarantee for rebellion. The best course of action is to ask your teenager to accept your values and explain your reasons for adopting them in your own life. You must show him how your values have worked for you and how they will apply to your teenager's life. If you embark on a shared process with your teenager that helps him form and discover his values for living, then you will establish yourself as his partner for life.

Your teenager needs clearly defined boundaries and accountability in the context of a loving relationship. This is the most common area where parents fall short in relating to their teenagers. Finding a balance is difficult, but failure to do so results in one of two extremes. One extreme holds both the boundaries and accountability too tightly, causing the teenager to chafe under the "mean rules" and ultimately rebel. The other extreme makes the boundaries so loose as to be non-existent, causing the teenager to self-develop. To help your teenager find and develop his values, you do not have to become a drill sergeant nor do you have to become so removed that he is on his own. In fact, the best way to establish boundaries and enforce accountability is to develop mutually agreed upon values. This takes work, and more importantly, it takes a relationship with your teenager!

The best way to establish boundaries
and enforce accountability is to
develop mutually agreed upon values.

Five Concepts Necessary for Successful Adult Living

By now I hope you understand the principle of transference. As the underlying theme of this book, it is the idea that your children will adopt and embrace the values and qualities actively demonstrated in your life.

You've heard the statement, "I'm sorry, I can't hear what you are saying. Your actions are speaking too loudly." This is the mantra of the teenage generation. It is a reminder that your values must be modeled for your children if you want them to transfer. *Your actions are a much more influential tutor than the instruction of your words or the concepts you believe but do not practice*! As I share these five concepts, it is important that you live them. If you do not, they will ring hollow with your teenager.

WE MUST HAVE A TRUE COMPREHENSION OF GOD IN OUR LIVES.

In the Gospel of Matthew, a religious leader asks Jesus, "Teacher, which is the greatest commandment in the law?" Jesus' answer is simple yet profound: "You

shall love the Lord your God with all your heart, with all
your soul, and with all your mind" (Matthew 22:36–37).
In other words, our love for God should permeate every
aspect of our lives. No situation, whether at home,
school, or work, is outside God's loving care and involvement. No scenario with family, friends, or those in
authority is beyond the scope of His interest.

It was this perspective that led to a conversation with
Tyler during his junior year of high school. I had noticed
his attitude had become careless regarding authority. He
was critical of teachers and the school administration.
He was grumpy about work and the people he worked
with, and I noticed he was driving too fast. I talked to
him about this carelessness, but he ignored it. After
a few days with no noticeable change, I brought it up
again and reminded him that God was interested in his
attitude toward authority. He took a little more notice
but not much. Then one Friday evening as I was coming
home from work, I noticed the strobe of flashing lights
ahead. A police officer had pulled two cars over on the
street leading to my house. As I drove down the street,
I recognized one of the cars as Tyler's. I parked behind
the police officer and walked to the driver's window of
Tyler's car. As I approached, I could see Tyler slide down
in the seat. I greeted him with "What's up, Tyler?" just as
the police officer returned with a ticket for drag racing.
The police officer asked, "You must be the dad?" I said,

"Yes, I am, and I appreciate the fine job you are doing. Is there anything you need me to do?" He said, "No, things are handled here." I turned to Tyler and said, "I will see you at home."

This incident was an object lesson in God's interest in the little details of Tyler's life. His careless attitude was noticed by me but ignored by him. God cared enough to insert a different authority to deal with his attitude before something more serious happened. God has ways to discipline us for our responses. For Tyler, it was a ticket, a court appearance, and a fine. My view of life tells me this was not bad luck or just the way life is, but it was God inserting Himself into the circumstances of life to deal with my son because He loves him!

During their teenage years, my children came to understand God's loving care and involvement in their lives. I transferred this concept to them through numerous situations like the one above in which I reminded them of God's interest and involvement in their lives. It was Jan's and my parenting that gave our children this perspective as they developed.

WE MUST SEE A GOD-CENTERED PURPOSE FOR OUR LIVES.

As a Christian, I see life as having purpose ordered by God. I see it in a macro sense in nature and world events, and I see it in a micro sense related to my life.

God created me (and you) with a purpose in mind.
Discovering our purpose is one of the most important
quests of life. Jeremiah 29:11 tells us about God's view of
us, that He knows us and thinks about us every moment.
He has plans for good and peace, plans for a future
and a hope and not plans of evil toward us. The most
important thing any of us can do is ask and answer the
question, "What does God want me to do?"

*The most important thing any of us
can do is ask and answer the question,
"What does God want me to do?"*

In the last chapter, I gave an account of how we
helped transfer this concept to our oldest son, Todd.
Beyond our influence we wanted his destiny in God
to be reinforced in a tangible way, which is why we
encouraged him to participate in the summer mission
trip to Ireland. We wanted to help our son discover
how God could lead and provide for something like
this if it is His desire and plan. To Todd, the trip
looked like it would be a waste of his summer—an
understandable teenage perspective. However,
supported by our guidance, this experience proved to
be an excellent tool for Todd to learn how to live with
God's plan in mind.

Our four children have each embraced the concept that God created them in their mother's womb and has a plan for their lives. Although this concept of a God-centered purpose for life was transferred to our children, they each grasped the concept in different ways unique to their own lives.

WE MUST UNDERSTAND THE IMPORTANCE OF A GOOD NAME.

Though it sometimes seems unfair, the truth is that we are known by the company we keep. Our reputation is influenced by the circle of our friends. We must guard against an attitude of pride or superiority that would lead us to think of ourselves as better than other people. The importance of a good name is not about race, economic standing, or social status. It is about *values*. Proverbs 22:1 says it this way: "A good name is to be chosen rather than great riches, loving favor rather than silver and gold." A good name is the reason we keep our word and choose as our close friends those who also value keeping their word. Although we are friendly to all people, we do not make close friendships with people of bad reputation unless they are willing to change their ways and be influenced by our values.

Simply stated, peer pressure is a powerful thing. If used properly, it makes us better. If peer pressure is ignored or taken lightly, it will result in our children being influenced to do wrong things by their friends. The influence of bad friends cannot be overestimated. The effect over time is what leads them to make bad life choices and ultimately what influences them to call what is good "bad" and what is bad "good." The apostle Paul writes, "Evil company corrupts good habits" (1 Corinthians 15:33). This truth is not age-specific but must be learned and embraced early in life. To do so will save a lot of heartache throughout life. We must monitor who our children spend time with and the impact of their friends on their behavior and attitudes.

WE MUST UNDERSTAND THAT CHARACTER, DILIGENCE, AND FAITHFULNESS ARE DEVELOPED THROUGH ADVERSITY.

In our community, there is a county fair each fall. We used to tell our children when they came home complaining about the unfairness of something that there is only one fair, and it is in the fall! I realize one of the responsibilities of a parent is to be the protector and defender of his children. I am not saying we should abandon that responsibility. However, a companion responsibility to protecting our children is building strength of character in them. Strength of character is the ability to do what is right when someone is looking and when no one is looking. Diligence is the capacity to keep doing something when the rewards are slow in coming. Faithfulness is the quality of accepting and acting with responsibility and loyalty in all the affairs of life.

> *Strength of character is the ability*
> *to do what is right when someone is*
> *looking and when no one is looking.*

The enemy to developing these qualities in our teenagers is a three-headed monster. First, it is the hurts from our past that cause us to make vows beginning with "I will never" or ending with "I will always." When some injustice touches our children, we can't help them deal with it through trust in God and forgiveness. Instead, we become offended for them and act based on the vow we made previously because of a painful experience in our own lives.

Second, it is attitudes of enabling that shield our children from every possible adversity of life. When our children come whimpering to us, we enable their inability to deal with life by acting on their behalf. The result is that we teach them there are no consequences for their behavior, leading them to believe life will always be fair, and if it is not, someone (other than God) will make it right for them. How does this fit with Jesus' statement in John 16 that the world will cause us tribulation? The comfort Jesus gives is the fact that He has overcome the world. *Jesus is the answer to every injustice.*

Finally, it is failed expectations placed on others which adversely touch our children. We expect a friend who is coaching to draft them, or we expect a business associate to hire and show favor to hire them. Unfulfilled expectations create disappointment that leads to hurt and offense, which, in turn, get in the way of our ability to help our children see God's hand in the circumstances that have disappointed them.

WE MUST UNDERSTAND THE IMPORTANCE OF RELATIONAL AND SOCIAL SKILLS.

The Bible indicates that God's plan for humanity incorporates all His work into *relationships*. It was because of God's love for us that Jesus came to redeem lost and fallen man. We reflect God's nature when we relate to each other with love and kindness. Imparting this concept begins by showing our children how to respond with honor and respect to adults and continues by showing them how to play with friends. It doesn't stop there but carries through each stage of development on their way to their teenage years, where they learn to respond in dating relationships. The dynamics of human relationship make it the most complicated relationship known to man. In order to relate in healthy ways, we must teach our children how to communicate, confront, resolve conflict, express affection, and be loyal and committed to family and friends.

A Concluding Thought

Parenting is not an exact science; it is a process. No parent is perfect because no human is perfect. When our children leave home to assume responsibility for their lives, we can guarantee a successful adjustment if we give them the tools. The concepts covered in this chapter are the tools teenagers need to succeed as adults. It is never too late to begin the process. Regardless of your children's ages or development stages, begin today to be an influential parent to them. Help your children progress into adulthood by teaching them to apply these important concepts to their lives.

15

Helping Teenagers Handle
Social Pressure

Do not be deceived:
Evil company corrupts good habits
(1 Corinthians 15:33).

G od created every person with appetites that
yearn to be satisfied. Appetites are intended to
drive us toward life-sustaining resources necessary
for health and growth. Some of these appetites are
familiar to us, but others may not have been identified, even though we have lived with them our entire
lives.

The five areas of appetite are food, sex, pleasure,
status, and God (or spiritual life). Since God created
these appetites, He also created the means by which they
can be satisfied in healthy and beneficial ways. For your
teenager to be prepared for the temptations, opportunities, and challenges of adulthood, he must learn how
to manage his appetites in emotionally, physically, and
spiritually healthy ways.

For your teenager to be prepared
for the temptations, opportunities,
and challenges of adulthood, he must
learn how to manage his appetites
in emotionally, physically,
and spiritually healthy ways.

From the time our children first interact with friends, they are thrust into situations that pressure them to respond to their developing appetites, often in ways that are unhealthy. The question facing them at each stage of development is the same one that faces us as adults: *Who or what will influence the decisions of my life*?

How will we satisfy the cravings of our appetites? Will the appetite craving fulfillment be satisfied by the quickest fix available? Will the appetite for pleasure be influenced by friends or be satisfied as God intended? Will the appetite for status or the appetite for sex be satisfied according to the accepted morals of our culture, or will these appetites be satisfied as God desires— through humility and hard work and within the context of a committed marriage relationship?

When our children first began playing with friends, we monitored the effects of their play on both their actions and their attitudes. If we found that our child's attitude was rebellious or disrespectful after playing with a friend, or his behavior was such that he knew we would not approve, we restricted or eliminated his play with that friend. It is our responsibility as parents to teach our children how to live out the biblical values we impart even in the face of pressure to act otherwise. At every stage of development, we must teach our children the best way to handle the pressure to act against their values, teaching them to fulfill appetites in healthy ways. If we fail to do this at the ages of four, five, and six years old, we have forfeited our prime opportunity to train these appetites. God never intended for us to wait to begin training our children to manage their appetites in their teenage years.

Jan and I were diligent to do this training with each of our children. The situations were different with each child, but the method was always the same. It was not our desire to dominate their lives but to make sure that the good habits we were seeking to develop in them were not corrupted or undone by the influence of friends or people who did not hold our same values. We could not let the worldly influences around them teach them how to satisfy their appetites. We had to be proactive in parenting our teenagers.

Sometimes the issue wasn't that our children's friends had different values. Their families often had the same values as ours. The issue was that our children and certain friends did not influence each other in good ways as they played together. We had to take action for their mutual benefit. Such was the case with one of Tyler's friends, Michael. Michael was a sweet, fun-loving boy who was pleasant to be around, and Jan and I were friends with his parents. Tyler and Michael played together from the time they were born; they were best friends. As they got older, they both became such active boys that my friend, Jimmy Evans, dubbed them the "hyper-twins."

About the time the "hyper-twins" turned eight years old, we began to notice that they got into mischief when they played together. For instance, the boys were left alone one day to play together while Michael's mom ran a short errand. They were playing in Michael's garage and found some cans of spray paint. In a playful moment, one of the boys removed the cap from one of the cans and sprayed its contents into the air. No harm was done, so the other boy did the same. This playful moment led to one boy spray painting a line on the wall, which led to the other boy copying with another line. They spent the next hour or so spray painting the garage walls with their eight-year-old version of graffiti art.

You can imagine the response of Michael's mom when she arrived home to find the boys' handiwork. Both boys knew better than to spray the garage wall with paint, but neither could stop the other from doing what they both knew was wrong. Their appetites for pleasure and status were being fulfilled through unhealthy behavior, and neither boy was influencing the other to do what they knew was right.

This was not a singular, isolated event but a growing trend that led us to decide that the boys could not play together again until they could influence each other's behavior in a positive way. I don't remember exactly how long it was before they were allowed to play together again, but I do remember that it was months, not just a few days.

A detailed explanation about their appetites was not a part of our teaching; only how to manage them. As parents, we knew their appetites were governing their behavior. We also knew that we had to teach our children to satisfy their appetites properly to get the behavior we knew was right. When Tyler and Michael resumed play, they did so with an awareness of their responsibility to be good influences on each other. They have remained good friends even to this day, and Michael was a groomsman in Tyler's wedding.

Addressing Temptations

Teenagers are presented with a variety of temptations as they grow up. A temptation is nothing more than an opportunity to satisfy an appetite—usually in an unhealthy way. We cannot ignore temptations or assume that because our children have the influence of the church in their lives, or because they have been raised in our home and know our values, that they will be able to resist either the temptations or the peer pressures that pull at them on a daily basis. *We must teach them how to satisfy their appetites in a godly, biblical, and healthy way.*

A temptation is nothing more than an opportunity to satisfy an appetite— usually in an unhealthy way.

Proactive parenting must take a position on drugs, premarital sex, alcohol, attitudes toward authority, and a whole host of other issues affecting life. We not only must take a position, but we must also communicate this position regularly to our children while we monitor their acceptance of our standards and their ability to stand firm in the face of temptation and pressure.

We cannot assume that other parents hold our same values or that they will be as vigilant in monitoring or enforcing them as we are. One of the steps Jan and I took as our children entered their teenage years was to enforce a "party policy." When one of our children came home and told us that he or she had been invited to a party at a friend's house, we asked to see the invitation. Without exception, we saw rolled eyes and a look as if we were from Mars. We were the old, out of touch people, unaware that teenagers do not send out formal invitations to parties. Their invitations are by word-of-mouth.

Although this is a common method of inviting friends to a party, our teenagers could not attend unless we had one of two things: a formal invitation or a conversation with the parents of the teenager having the party. We wanted to make sure the parents were aware of the party and confirm they were going to be chaperoning what was taking place. Our goal was not to prevent our children from attending parties but to help them avoid situations that were too pressure-filled for them to handle and to teach them how to have fun in a healthy way. We consistently applied this policy, and after a few times, our teenagers knew without exception what was needed to get our okay. The parties they did attend were properly chaperoned where teenagers were having fun without breaking the law or hurting themselves.

In Chapter 4, I referred to my position on drinking as I related a story about my oldest son and a souvenir beer bottle he brought home. I thought it better to give a more thorough explanation of my position in this chapter rather than explain myself in the context of the story. Substance abuse in many forms is something our children will be exposed to, and they must have an answer. They don't need to experiment on their own to find it—it is our parental responsibility to help them. This is why it is important for us to help them understand their appetites and to work with them to find God's method of satisfying them.

First, let me say I believe in having fun. I enjoy life to its fullest, and I want my children to do the same. However, I do not hold to the belief that part of growing up is "sowing your wild oats" in order to find yourself. I don't think you have to experience something to avoid it. For instance, I have never been in jail, and I have no desire to be in jail. I haven't had to experience jail to form this opinion.

Parental attitudes regarding substance abuse vary based on personal experience and personal use. There are a variety of things teenagers may illegally use and abuse, such as drugs, alcohol, glue, and cigarettes. While not exhaustive, this list does represent things that, as parents, we want our children to learn about and handle healthily and responsibly. Parental involvement is not only necessary; it is essential in guiding our children to healthy and responsible behavior. We must teach them how to satisfy their appetites for pleasure and status among their friends.

Once again, we must "walk the walk" before we "talk the talk" when relating principles to our children. This is true for how we handle substances as well. Have you learned to satisfy your appetites in a healthy way? Do you model this for your children to see? How can we guide our children related to substances if we abuse them ourselves?

My response to drinking alcohol is based on an overall response to substance abuse and an understanding of how to satisfy an appetite for pleasure and status in a way sanctioned by God. It is not based on religious feelings of performance or emotions of guilt; it is based on my value system. Although my values are founded on the principles of the Bible, they were impacted and shaped by personal experiences as well.

My first exposure to drinking came when I was in junior high school. In Sunday school each week, the high school boys would tell wild stories of their drunken escapades from Friday and Saturday nights. It always struck me as inconsistent that they would tell these stories while carrying their Bibles and talking about God. Hypocrisy is a religious coat that Jesus opposed wherever He encountered it because it replaces a personal relationship with God with a false front. We certainly don't want to wear that coat nor pass it on for our children to wear.

I was raised in a home where drinking was accepted. When I began high school, my dad sat me down and told me that I would be exposed to alcohol. He asked me to come to him if I was ever interested in trying it, and he would give me what I wanted from his supply at home. He told me he would rather do that than have me experiment on my own and drive under the influence of alcohol. I never took my dad up on his offer, but during my high school years, I knew the offer was on the table. It may have been part of the reason I never became interested. I knew I did not have to try alcohol in secret to learn what it was all about.

One other experience influenced the way I viewed alcohol. The dad of one of my close high school friends was an alcoholic. I saw firsthand the pain my friend experienced when his dad disappeared on multi-day drinking binges. I never accompanied my friend when he went to find his dad and bring him home, but I imagined how awful that would be. I decided I wanted nothing to do with something so destructive. There had to be a different way to satisfy an appetite for pleasure.

As I have been exposed to different cultures around the world and have grown in my knowledge of the Bible, my experiences have joined with what I now know are the Bible's parameters on this subject. More important than my experiences are the Bible's instructions related to these appetites and the healthy ways to satisfy them.

Alcohol and drugs, in my view, are risks. When people drink or take drugs, they risk addiction, their reputation, their employment, and their family. They risk everything important in life. Life is filled with risks, and many risks are out of our control. We have to depend on God to protect us from the risks that are beyond our control. But I see the risk related to drugs and alcohol as something I can control by the choices I make and the lifestyle I live.

In teaching my children about their appetites and the temptations to satisfy them, I shared the Bible's perspective along with my experiences. As I taught my children, I understood that my perspective was my own—I knew they would have to make their own decisions related to the values they held for their lives. I understood that ultimately their decisions would be between them and God.

It was my desire that they would agree with my values and adopt them as their own, but I could not make them do so. I shared my perspective to give them guidance, but each had to decide for his or her own life the way they would find pleasure, satisfaction, and purpose. However, as they made their decisions, I wanted them to talk with me about what had been decided so that I would know what to expect and so that I could keep each accountable for his or her decision.

As part of forming their decisions, I gave them what I believed was the biblical perspective on satisfying their appetites in a healthy manner so they could factor that into their choices. Regardless of their decisions, whether they were the same as mine or not, they knew they would have to live within biblical boundaries to experience God's blessing in their lives. Here are the biblical guidelines I gave them:

Be submitted to the governing authorities and their laws (Romans 13:1).

This means no teenage drinking. Underage drinking and illicit drug use are against the laws of the United States.

Consider the influence your action might have on others before you act, even if it is within biblical boundaries.

Paul gives a charge in his letter to the Romans that Christians are not to live for themselves (Romans 14:7). It is my experience that when a person wants his life to be an example of his love for Christ, the good intention loses its influence when associated with self-gratification and personal indulgences. Even though you may have freedom to indulge within proper boundaries (to drink, for instance, if you are of legal age and do not drink to excess), someone may observe your example and use it to justify their wrong behavior. Or another person may witness your behavior and be offended. In his first letter to the Corinthians, Paul encourages them to be sensitive to matters of conscience in the people around them. Since it is difficult to know who is watching and how they might perceive your behavior, even if it is within legal or biblical parameters, I choose not to drink (1 Corinthians 8:9–13).

Your reputation is important for God's further use and placement of you in responsible positions of authority in His kingdom.

Consider the impact of your behavior on your reputation. The qualifications for church leadership raise a high standard related to many areas of life and personal conduct. For instance, the Bible states that an elder must not be given to wine (1 Timothy 3:3). I told my children that if they aspired to leadership in God's kingdom and in His church, they must sacrifice personal liberties and conduct themselves in a manner that reflects God's nature and character.

The appearance of wrongdoing can create as many problems as a wrong act itself.

It is important to consider *how* and *where* your fun takes place. When the Bible presents drinking in an acceptable light, it is related to celebration. Practically speaking, when our children came of legal age to drink, we did not forbid them to do so because the Bible does not forbid drinking. It does say that the alcohol-related celebrating cannot be immoral, involve drunkenness, or include carousing (Galatians 5:19).

Experimenting with pleasure or hedonistic self-gratification is dangerous.

If we seek God, we will find pleasure in Him. The Greek word for sorcery is *pharmica,* which we translate into "pharmacy." Nowhere in the Bible is illicit drug use condoned in any form; in fact, a case can be made that it is associated with idol worship. While we use drugs for medical purposes, we do not experiment with them, and they are never to control us. They are not to be abused for self-gratification or pleasure.

I told my children that if they chose not to embrace my perspective as their own, I would be disappointed, but I would always love them. The choice was theirs, and I would respect it and them. However, regardless of their choice, I taught them that they were not free to live outside of the biblical parameters listed above. All of our children have embraced as their own the values Jan and I have taught and modeled.

A Concluding Thought

It is not my purpose in this chapter to present my perspective as something you must embrace. Rather, my purpose is to remind you that as parents, we must give our children guidance in how to conduct their lives and satisfy their God-given appetites. We must challenge our children, through our own behavior and the values we transfer to them, to live a life of influence for God.

We must challenge our children,
through our own behavior and the
values we transfer to them,
to live a life of influence for God.

What I would say to all parents is this: you must define, communicate, and model your values clearly for your children to understand and embrace them as their own. Your children need guidance as they form their moral and spiritual values for living. To help them, you must have searched the Scriptures and defined God's perspective on the issues. You also must be proactive with your children regarding the pressures and temptations they face and provide guidance as they form their responses.

Successful parenting of teenagers involves teaching them to fulfill their emerging and raging appetites in godly and healthy ways. Have you learned to do this in your own life? Are you proactively involved with your teenagers? They need your active involvement and instruction as they finish their preparation for adulthood. Even if your children are grown, it's not too late to begin influencing them to satisfy their appetites in godly and healthy ways. Your influence as a parent and grandparent has long-lasting generational effects. You can act now to be the influence God desires.

Section Four

Protecting Standards

16

Responding to Wayward Children

Remember the big picture: It ain't over 'til it's over!

When Jan and I began our family, I assumed that my parental responsibilities would be over for the most part once my children reached adulthood. I was mistaken. Over the years, I've found the statement "once a parent, always a parent" to be true. Although parenting responsibilities change as children get older, they never completely disappear.

Both the Bible and archaeological discoveries from past civilizations provide models that confirm the premise of lifetime parenting. Before the advent of planes, trains, and automobiles, when mobility was limited, people naturally assumed that their families would grow together. In Jesus' day, people were born, married, and buried all within a few hundred square miles. Travel was not only slow by today's standards—it was dangerous. Families stayed together, affording each new generation the influence and example of the previous ones.

Today's society offers more choices, often to the peril of the family unit. Children grow up and leave home to pursue education, build careers, and start families, often moving hundreds of miles away from brothers, sisters, parents, grandparents, aunts, uncles, and cousins. This diminished family influence allows pressures and temptations now to come to adult children more easily. Without the network of family support, wrong influences pressure them with greater success, turning them away from the values that their parents worked hard to instill. As they search for identity and purpose, they are left alone to respond to destructive influences, competing for their lives and forced to ride out turbulent waves of pressures and temptations on their own.

The previous two generations have particularly suffered in this way. As mobility has increased, families have fractured. More than half of all marriages fail today. Children are left without the nurturing influence of the family. Even those who are nurtured are often pulled from the stability and strength of their immediate and extended families as they roam further and further to pursue pleasure, education, and careers. When adult children hit turbulent waters and their lives are turned upside down by divorce, job loss, drug abuse, or any number of factors, they often find themselves without the support and accountability of their families. Increasingly, we see young adults in crisis—victims of a mobile society with changing values and shifting morality—returning home to the place of their roots for support and regrouping.

What are we as parents to do when our troubled young adults return home? Receive them with open arms? We raised them once. Is it our responsibility to do it a second or third time?

Responding to Wrong Behavior

Knowing how to respond to adult children in crisis is particularly difficult when the situation is a result of the wrong choices they have made. Instinct tells us that it might be best for them to pay for their mistakes, especially when they have either not sought our input or flat-out rejected it as they created their mess. In these situations, we may feel justified in being critical, or we may feel it necessary to invoke tough love because we have been rejected and are disappointed in their choices. A response that says, "You got yourself into this mess; you can get yourself out of it," seems to be the right solution. But is it? "How else will they learn their lessons?" you ask.

Our loving intention is to drive home a point. We want our adult children to wake up and learn from their mistakes. We want to make sure they do not repeat their blunders, so we attempt to control and fix their wrong behavior, and we often do it with a condescending, "I told you so" attitude. *This response will not change our children's behavior; instead, it will erect barriers that keep them removed from our love and the influence they need.*

What is the correct way to respond? What is a parent to do? Knowing how to respond requires wisdom. What seems natural by instinct often does not reflect God's nature; it just vents our frustration. The way we respond cannot enable our adult children's wrong behavior, but neither should it completely reject them, leaving them no avenue for return. Looking to God as our model, here is what we must do: we must be gracious and kind yet not compromise the standard of our beliefs. We must allow them the freedom of choice and be willing to forgive and restore relationship when there is a right response, not holding their mistakes over their heads indefinitely. Of course, this is easier said than done.

> *The way we respond cannot enable our adult children's wrong behavior, but neither should it completely reject them, leaving them no avenue for return.*

Dwayne came to my office brokenhearted by the choices his son, Kelly, was making. He was at a loss as to how to respond. Kelly had filed for divorce after six years of marriage. Dwayne knew that Kelly and his wife, Carrie, were struggling; he had observed increased tension between them. But he struggled to support the decision Kelly made to leave the marriage that also included two children.

Dwayne tried to talk his son into taking another route in solving his problems, but Kelly could not move his thinking from his decision to divorce his wife. In addition to filing for divorce, Kelly quit a stable, well-paying job and planned to pursue a dream of owning his own business. His hobby was motorcycles, and he told Dwayne that he intended to buy a motorcycle shop and race motorcycles. Kelly did not care who didn't like it—his mind was made up.

Dwayne came to me to discuss what he should do to help Kelly. This is the type of dilemma many parents find themselves in with their adult children. As parents, should we attempt to force them to do what we think is best? If we disagree with their decisions, do we continue a relationship with them, never making their decision an issue between us?

Each situation requires God's wisdom. There is great emotional trauma in these circumstances for all involved, especially when one parent wants to exercise tough love and the other wants to extend open arms to the child regardless of their mistakes. My counsel to Dwayne was to follow the path of the prodigal son's father. I encouraged him not to attempt to control or manipulate his son. I acknowledged how hard it would be for Dwayne and his wife to release their son to make decisions that would bring hurt now and possibly regret later. I advised him not to cut off his relationship with Kelly but also not to compromise what he felt was right in order to maintain the relationship.

I reminded Dwayne that God allows each of us to make our own choices—to follow Him or go our own way—even though He knows the full and final destruction associated with the wrong decision. He stands ready to receive us if or when we return to Him broken by the results of our decision.

Prayer is the appropriate place for us to pour out our concerns, frustrations, and passionate pleas for action. God is the only one who knows all things. He can arrange circumstances to apply the right pressure to jog our adult children's thinking in a way that does not violate their freedom of choice but works to change their hearts, returning them to what they know is right.

Fathers Build Bridges for Their Children

The parable of the prodigal son is found in Luke 15. It is the story of a young son who rejects his father's advice and makes a series of wrong choices, only to return home after making a mess of his life. This biblical story could have been drawn from many family situations in America today. Its theme is as current as this morning's news.

The story Jesus tells is a picture of how God the Father responds to His children. The account provides two key revelations for parents. First, it reveals the way to respond to actions of independence and what seems to be wayward behavior in our adult children. Second, it provides parents a model for relating to their adult children. It treats the relationship in such a way that it builds and maintains a bridge for the adult children's return back to the values imparted to them while they were at home. Proverbs 22:6 tells us that if we raise our children according to godly standards and values, they will not depart from this training when they are old. *They may divert, but they won't depart*! That is a promise to hold on to!

The story goes like this: The younger of two sons approaches his father and asks for an early distribution of the inheritance coming to him. The son's request carries with it a rejection of the family and implies a loathing attitude toward the family business. He wants to head out on his own.

The father apportions his possessions, giving the youngest son what is rightfully his. The son promptly leaves home and through a series of bad decisions, wastes his inheritance on riotous or prodigal living.

Whatever prodigal living might have been, it is safe to
say the son was making choices that were not consistent with the values his father had imparted to him.
After some time, the wayward son spent all his inheritance and made a mess of his life, a path not unlike
the one some young people take on their journey to
adulthood.

The waves of life shipwrecked the young son, and he
found himself in a desperate situation. The story says,
"When he came to himself, he said, '... I will arise and go
to my father'" (Luke 15:17–18). In other words, the son
took an inventory of his life and the mess he had created
and realized it was not what he wanted. He decided
to go home. He hoped his father would take him back
as a servant and provide him with room and board in
exchange for work.

According to custom, the father was not obligated to
help his son since he had disassociated himself from the
family by taking his inheritance and departing. In fact,
his father was entitled to treat him as dead, to respond
as though he never existed. The prodigal son would have
been aware of his father's right, yet he reasoned that if
his father would take him back—not as a son but as a
lowly servant—it would be better than the situation he
had made for himself.

What is the responsibility of a father to his children?
When is it fulfilled? The answer to that question forms

the foundation for the response the father made to his prodigal son. It is the answer we need to embrace as we respond to the wayward behavior of our children.

A father's primary responsibility is to reveal God to his children by teaching them about God and His ways and helping them find eternal purpose for their lives. The fulfillment of this responsibility takes consistent input and guidance throughout their lives. All children search for identity and purpose. Some break away from the guidance of their parents as they search. A wise father will build and maintain the bridge necessary for his children to come home.

A father's primary responsibility is to reveal God to his children by teaching them about God and His ways and helping them find eternal purpose for their lives.

When Children Return Home

In the parable, the father not only took his wayward son back, but he also restored his rights as a son, receiving him with celebration. This response is uncharacteristic of many fathers who have had children go their own ways, especially when the children's choices have ended in disaster. The father's response serves as a pattern to be followed by all fathers because it is a representation of God's response to each of us. Notice that the father's response to his wayward son accomplished four things:

- It recognized his son's need to find significance.
- It allowed his son a process of discovery in his search.
- It acknowledged his son's ability to make choices but refused to enable his wrong behavior.
- It kept the focus on the completed search and the enduring fruit it would produce.

When we learn to incorporate this four-fold pattern of response, we will further God's work in our children's lives and help them discover their purpose, even if their search takes a rocky road. Let's look more closely at the father's response and what it accomplished.

THE SEARCH FOR SIGNIFICANCE

The search for significance is common to all humanity. It is the homing mechanism in the heart of man, designed to motivate him to search for God. Discovering the purpose for which we were created is the only way to satisfy fully the search for personal significance in our lives. Our fullest and deepest purpose can only be found through a relationship with God. The process of discovery has many roads; we do not all arrive by the same one. Regardless of the road taken, everyone hungers to know his or her purpose.

Discovering the purpose for which we were created is the only way to satisfy fully the search for personal significance in our lives.

It is critical for parents to understand that God has built the desire to know one's purpose into the human fabric. Personal contentment and happiness are directly linked to the purpose for which we were created. Therefore, helping our children discover their significance is critical. God created children with unique personalities, physical attributes, and abilities. He has a specific plan for each of their lives.

As our children search for significance, we must understand that the discovery process is not always smooth, convenient, or the method of our choosing. *We must also remember that our children's self-esteem is closely connected to the discovery process.* Just like us, our children seek to satisfy their needs for identity, purpose, acceptance, and security. Their search begins by identifying mechanisms that supply these basic needs, and the fulfillment of these needs provides a foundation for significance. The standards and training we model and transfer to our children help them know the good and acceptable ways to satisfy their needs.

In the story, the father releases his son, without apparent resistance, to search for his own significance. Our sons and daughters will not find their significance in the fulfillment of plans, goals, and desires we have determined as best for their lives, regardless of how noble they seem. They must identify their plans, goals, and desires for themselves. Our role is to provide encouragement and guidance for them in the process of their search.

Several years ago, a young, single woman lived with us. She was a wonderful blessing to our family. She had completed college and was working as a nurse.

One evening as we were talking about her frustrations with work, the discussion turned to her choice of nursing as a career. To my surprise, I found that she hated nursing. She only did it because it was her degree field. I asked, "If you hate nursing, why did you choose it?" She told me it was not her choice; her parents picked it for her. They told her nursing would provide her with a career that would enable her to support herself and not depend on anyone else.

I understand the care and concern behind this parental logic; however, there was one fatal flaw— they did not allow their daughter to discover and hold this purpose as her own. They determined what was best for her without considering what was in her heart. This young woman was out of college, working in a career she hated, living away from her parents, and supporting herself, yet she was nowhere close to finding and understanding her personal significance. How could she know or find her significance when her parents had never validated her identity as unique before God?

The first work of God in our lives is to guide us to discover our uniqueness in Him. Therefore, *our first responsibility as parents is to help our children find their significance.* One way we do this is by communicating to them that they have a unique identity created by God in their mother's womb.

During the children's developmental years, we must help them define their purpose and guide them in their search for significance. As they mature into adults, we can pray for them, encourage them, and support their search for the most important ingredient in personal satisfaction—the knowledge of their created purpose.

The process requires that we recognize their right to choose a road we would not choose for them if that is their desire. Even though we anticipate the pain their choice will potentially cause them, we cannot force them to do what we believe best because this would violate their God-given right to choose. God does not force us to choose His way, even though He knows the benefit of such a decision. He allows us to make the choice not to follow His will, to His grief and to our eternal detriment.

People who feel significant have discovered three important factors. First, they have made a connection between their lives and something bigger, a grand purpose or scheme to which they can contribute. When we help our children discover God and His plan for their lives, they connect with Him and embrace something bigger than their own lives. God's plan and purpose have eternal implications for every person. True significance can only be identified in connection with Him.

> *God's plan and purpose have eternal implications for every person. True significance can only be identified in connection with Him.*

Second, people who feel significant have discovered their personal abilities or gifts, and they use them to contribute to the fulfillment of the bigger plan to which they are connected. Just connecting to something bigger is not enough to define their significance. It must be accompanied by a sense of personal contribution. They must know that their personal contribution is important in the grand scheme of things.

Third, people who feel significant have had their talents and contributions validated by another person. Parents or other people of influence must validate their purpose and acknowledge that the gifts and abilities they have contribute to a bigger purpose in an important way. If a person has the first and second parts of significance but never receives validation from people of influence in his life, he will struggle to believe and fully accept the significance of his contribution.

THE PROCESS OF SEARCHING

Finding significance is a process that unfolds over time, often over a period of years. The process can be difficult, and if the person is rebellious, it will be painful, perhaps even tragic. Aware of this reality, some parents refuse to empower their children to search.

The prodigal son's father empowered his search for significance. When his son requested his inheritance, the father granted his request. We can only assume that he knew a lecture would not change his son's mind. The request was a part of his son's search for purpose and significance. The boy had determined that what he wanted could not be found in the shadow of his brother or the confines of the family business. So, the father empowered his search.

The father empowered his son in two important ways. The first was financial empowerment through the

provision of the son's inheritance. Why do you suppose
the father gave his son an early inheritance? Do you
think he had a clue as to how his son would use it? Surely
if he had known, he would not have given it to his son to
waste. Wouldn't a loving father decline such a request?

The father's view of inheritance is different from our
view in western civilization. Our modern view is that
inheritance is something we leave to our children to
bless them with a better life. Using this logic, it makes
no sense to give an inheritance when it will not be
used to make a better life. This is the majority opinion
among parents today. But the attitude of the father in
the parable is different. In Jesus' day, an inheritance
was something that was owed. It was an investment in a
son's search for significance. If the father's investment
resulted in his son finding purpose and significance, it
would be a great investment, producing a result greater
than any material accumulation an extra few years of
waiting might produce.

The resource the son received in the form of his inheritance was secondary to the support he received in the
form of his father's permission to fail in his search. When
we as parents recognize our responsibility to help our
children find significance, then investing in their search
has a worthwhile purpose. By giving the inheritance with
no conditions attached, the father acknowledged and
empowered his son's freedom of choice.

Our children are not empowered to search if they cannot fail. I am not suggesting that failure is the best method for finding significance. Through years of investment, I have sought to guide my children in their search so that they would not have to hit rock bottom before finding their purpose. However, had they chosen the harder route and ignored my guidance, I would have had to let them go.

Failure brought the prodigal son to an understanding of his own identity, gave him a desire to be connected to something bigger than himself, and helped him understand the value of being connected to family. The inheritance was wasted, but something greater was gained.

My dad did this for me when I was younger. He encouraged me to follow my heart, leave his company, and step into vocational ministry. Although it was not his plan for me to be in ministry and even though it carried the risk of failure, my dad supported my decision and gave me the freedom to fail in my search.

EMPOWERMENT OR ENABLEMENT

How do we support our children's search for significance without enabling their wrong behavior or poor choices? How do we provide resources and not compromise our beliefs and values? If a child is not living or acting according to our standards, is the search invalidated, or is this behavior part of the searching process? These are important questions that must be answered so we can know how to guide our children in their search.

In a positive sense, enablement and empowerment could be used synonymously. However, I want to talk with you for a minute about enablement that is negative and unhealthy, meaning it gives authority to do wrong through tacit approval of the values behind the behavior. This enablement will not have a guiding result but instead acts as negligent oversight.

Considering this definition of enablement, how would you respond to the following question: Is providing resources for your child's search for significance equal to or the same as approving of his behavior? Is it the same as accepting his values? Or is it acknowledging his self-governance?

If supporting his search equates to approving of wrong behavior or accepting alternative values as the foundation for determining behavior, then it would be irresponsible to give support. But is that right? Did the father in the story give authority for his son's riotous living or accept his son's values for behavior by supporting his search? The answer is NO.

He empowered his son's search, but he did not enable his son's bad behavior and wrong choices by sending additional support when the son's funds ran out. Acknowledging his son's right and responsibility to govern himself, the father gave his son his inheritance and made him responsible for how it was spent.

Let me put this discussion in another context. Imagine you encounter a homeless person on a street corner who is holding a sign that reads, "Vet out of work. Need food. Can you spare some change?" You feel compassion for the person and reach into your pocket and give him some money. Does your act of compassion give him the authority to beg or associate you with his values for behavior? The answer is no. By responding with compassion to a need, you have neither automatically approved the behavior nor associated yourself with the values.

Consider another situation. You are an employer, and you have an employee whose personal behavior away from work does not please you or represent your values. When you hand him his paycheck, are you agreeing with your employee's behavior away from your workplace or the values that form the basis for his actions? Again, the answer is no. When you hand him his paycheck, you are giving him something that is due to him in exchange for the work he has done. When you give him his check, he is responsible for how it is spent. You are acknowledging his responsibility for self-governance.

We should support our children's search for purpose and significance without enabling them in an unhealthy way. When our support is a response that acknowledges their responsibility for self-governance, it is an empowering response. This is what our children need.

I grew up with an awareness that I was entitled to certain benefits just because I was born into the Lane family. The benefits were based upon my blood relationship, not upon my behavior. My dad often told me something like this: "If you rob a bank or murder someone, I am still going to love you. I will always love you. You will always be a part of this family. I may not like what you do, but you will always be my son."

Regardless of my behavior, my dad will always be my dad. This idea is a biblical concept as well. In fact, the whole idea of inheritance in the Bible is based on relationship, not merit. Consider for a moment the benefits your children are entitled to simply because they were born into your family—benefits such as unconditional love, security, food, clothing, etc. Beyond these benefits guaranteed to all family members are conditional blessings, which are based upon approval and agreement with the choices and direction of each person.

The father's response to his prodigal son's request bears wisdom that we can use for ourselves. First, when the search involves a departure from parental values, the financial support is for a defined amount. The father determined what was due to his son in the amount of the inheritance and gave it to him—no monthly support and no further response were sent to the son when the money was gone.

When does support become unhealthy enablement for a child's behavior? When you give and it is wasted, and then you give again, and it is wasted again. By continuing to be an unending resource of material support, you enable your child's rebellion. His riotous lifestyle is no longer a search; it is a decision that has resulted in rebellion against you and God. To provide continued support for this behavior is merely prolonging the process of him coming to his senses.

A Concluding Thought

The final thought I draw from the story of the prodigal son is this: *it is never too late to do what is right.* If you have a wayward child, he has been in God's care all along. You can begin today to release your child to find significance by freeing him from your criticisms, threats of rejection, or attempts of control.

As you have read this chapter, you may have been convicted by the realization that you have not fulfilled your responsibility as a parent to help your child find identity and purpose through connection to God's sovereign plan for his life. It might be that throughout the discussion in this chapter, you have become aware of how little affirmation or support you have given your child in his search for personal significance. It is not too late. You can start today.

Simply ask God to give you insight and wisdom on exactly what to do. I know He will direct you and give you the grace to accomplish this important work. By faith, you can anticipate the completion of your child's search, believing God to bring him to his senses. During the process, I encourage you to hold celebration in your heart and expect your child's return. Remember the big picture: It ain't over 'til it's over!

17

Partnering with God through Prayer

The prayers of a father have great power to influence
his children and future generations.

T he bedrock of my philosophy of rearing children
is my conviction that parenting at its core is a
partnership with God.

As a father, I am God's representative to my children.
I am an extension and reflection of Him to them. If I
detach from my children, they will see God as detached.
If I act bored with them, they will see God as bored with
them. If I am present, involved, and interested, they will
grow up with the correct perception of God. *The kind of
father I am will form the basis for my children's understanding of God's love and care.*

Remember the story from Chapter 1 about the college
professor's survey? After a whole semester of Bible
study, his students' perceptions of God were still direct
reflections of their relationships with their fathers! Nine
weeks of instruction and 27 classes of Bible teaching,

homework, and tests had not changed this. The students' home environments and the demonstrations of their fathers' love, or lack thereof, were stronger factors than all the hours of teaching and study.

The impact of parental influence on children is profound—by God's design. He never intended for parenting to be a solely human endeavor. He designed parenting to be a partnership between Himself (the Divine Creator) and parents (His agents of procreation). To be partners with God—to be His representatives—we must pray.

> *To be partners with God—to be His representatives—we must pray.*

Now, the subject of prayer can evoke a variety of thoughts, so let me briefly explain what I mean by prayer. *Prayer is our connective link to God.* It is neither a religious duty nor a sequence of magical words. It is not something that only pastors and priests can do. Prayer is a conversation with God that flows out of a relationship with Him.

We communicate with God through prayer just like we would converse with anyone with whom we have a relationship. As a father, I am motivated to pray because

I know prayer is part of my responsibility as God's partner. Through prayer, God and I communicate about how to mold, nurture, and develop my children. Prayer waters and fertilizes the principles of life and qualities of character that I am planting deep into the fertile soil of my children's hearts.

Imparting the principles of God into life's learning situations is a process much like farming. To achieve the maximum results from his labor, a farmer must plant the right seed in the right season. Otherwise, his crops will not grow. If he plants the right seed in the right season, watering and fertilizing will determine the quantity and quality of the fruit produced.

It is the same with our children. We must plant seeds in their lives. We must also realize that our attention to the process will determine the quantity and quality of the fruit produced. Without watering and fertilizing the principles of God through patient application, watchful oversight, and faithful prayer, the results will be less than desired.

Even though a farmer picks the right seed and plants it at the right time, he must water and fertilize it, or it will be stunted in its growth, producing little or no fruit. It is the same with our parenting. Even if we are diligent in imparting the right biblical principles, and even if we apply them with patient oversight, the effectiveness of our work diminishes without prayer.

Prayer waters the principles we impart into our children's hearts and produces the greatest amount of fruit. Without prayer, our efforts will produce weak results. Prayer is the recognition and extension of our partnership with God to raise and influence our children.

> *Prayer is the recognition and extension*
> *of our partnership with God to raise*
> *and influence our children.*

Where to Begin

You may have children who are elementary age or teenagers or adults with families of their own. No matter how old they are, it is never too late to start praying for them.

I love the phrase that a preacher used to begin his radio program: "God is still on the throne, and prayer changes things!" This statement embodies the two foundational stones on which prayer is based. "God is still on the throne" means that He is in control. No situation or circumstance is a surprise to Him or beyond His power to change. "Prayer changes things" means that my petitions to God make a difference. God listens and responds to my requests.

How to Pray

When I pray for my children, I ask God to bless them, to lead them into the fullness of His purpose for their lives, and to give me wisdom for decisions regarding them.

When our oldest daughter, Lisa, was approaching her sixteenth birthday, she began lobbying for a car. We told her that we would pray with her about it. After praying for a few weeks, we received a car for Lisa from a family member. Jan and I were thrilled by what we recognized as an answer to prayer. Lisa was less thrilled; she was thinking of something different than a 1985 Pontiac 4-door sedan that only had AM radio. She acted like it would be better to walk than to drive an "old person's car."

Her attitude reflected what many teenagers might feel if they had a choice of what car they were going to drive. We gave Lisa our perspective: God had supplied the car for her, and maybe the reason she got this particular car was to deal with an attitude of pride. We taught and modeled for our children the belief that God's nature is to bless us, and it is His great joy to give us the desires of our hearts. But He is first a good Father and will not give us gifts that foster qualities or behaviors that are harmful to us.

I told Lisa that I believed God would not provide another car for her until she changed her attitude and could demonstrate the change in the way she accepted and cared for the car God had supplied. To her credit, she did change her attitude. She subdued the pride that sought to make her hold her identity in a "thing," like the car.

Lisa drove her car for almost a year with a changed attitude. About a month before her seventeenth birthday, she asked if she and her mother could look at a car she saw for sale in the newspaper. I said yes but cautioned her not to get her hopes up about a new car. The car Lisa looked at was a red 1991 Mitsubishi Eclipse. She fell in love with the car and asked if I would look at it and test-drive it, which I did. It was a cute car, but it had high mileage, and the asking price was too high. As we drove home, I told Lisa I did not feel it was the car for her. She was disappointed but understood.

Jan and I talked about getting Lisa another car, and we decided to call a friend in the auto body repair business to see if he had anything that might fit our need and budget. He said he had just finished one and thought it would be perfect for a teenage girl. On my way home from work the next day, I drove by his shop. Right in front, shining in the sunlight, was a red 1990 Mitsubishi Eclipse, almost identical to the one Lisa and I test-drove. This one had been in an accident, but my friend bought it and repaired the damage. It looked perfect. I asked him if I could take it for a test-drive and have a car dealer examine it. He gave his okay. Everything looked great, and we negotiated a sales price pleasing to us both.

It was just two days before Lisa's birthday, so I took the car back to the car dealer for a tune-up and oil change. Then I picked it up after work on the night of her birthday. We had planned a birthday dinner with the family. I pulled up in front of the house, parked in the driveway, and casually walked in the front door. While the other family members waited in hiding, I asked Lisa to come downstairs. I told her I had something for her out front. She raced down the stairs and flew out the door. When she saw the car, she stopped dead in her tracks. She started jumping up and down, screaming of course. By this time all the family was out front to see the presentation and Lisa's reaction. She ran to the car and danced a full circle around it, screaming and shouting the whole time. Then she ran to Jan and me with hugs of joy and excitement. God had given her the desire of her heart. There was just an interim step in the process. He had answered her prayer and ours while correcting an attitude of pride in her heart.

I started praying like this for my children when they were young and continue to pray blessings over them even now that they are adults. As my children have matured through the stages of life, my prayers have changed accordingly. For instance, when they were born, they were in their most dependent stage.

I prayed over them as I rocked them to sleep, asking God to give them good health and strength all the days of their lives. My prayer was for their hearts always to be turned toward Him so that they never walked in rebellion. I asked for wisdom and guidance to be a good parent and to teach my children God's ways. I asked for help to live as a model of consistent and genuine love for God, even as I expressed my love for my children. I asked God to show me His will for my life and to enable me to be obedient to His leading, as a model for my children to follow.

As my children matured, prayer covered every situation they encountered. Problems with friends, academic struggles, teacher difficulties, and personality and attitude problems were all covered in prayer. Opportunities such as trying out for an athletic team, for a starting position, for cheerleader, for choir, or applying for jobs were all covered in prayer. The older our children became, the greater their needs—in a monetary sense as well as a spiritual one. We prayed for emotional, physical, spiritual, and financial needs, no matter what they were. Through prayer, God provided college tuition and vehicles when we had no way to supply those things. He opened doors of opportunity and protected our children from physical harm.

In these situations, our human perspective is limited. It is easy to measure each circumstance by its immediate impact, but there is so much more to consider, so much more we do not know. For instance, if my child makes the team and becomes a starter, what will be the effects of this opportunity? What factors will influence him? Will he be strong enough to stand against temptations and pressures or will he be led astray? The answers to these questions lie outside my knowledge as a parent but not outside God's infinite knowledge. That is what He is all about. I can cast my cares upon Him because I am convinced He cares for me and for my children! I pray for opportunities and ask God to direct the outcome as He knows best.

Even though I may think an opportunity is wonderful and positive, God may see it differently because He knows its future effect. Some opportunities never materialize because He has other plans that do not include the particular opportunity at hand. In His all-knowing wisdom, God sees opportunities in the light of His purpose for my children, and He knows which ones will lead to the fulfillment of that purpose and which ones will not.

We must trust the outcome of situations we hold in prayer into His care. Prayer requires trust and confidence that God will uphold His end of the partnership. Don't be hesitant or embarrassed to pray. In real terms, prayer is communication with our Partner in parenting.

Prayer requires trust and confidence
that God will uphold His end of the
partnership.

Prayer Journal

As my children matured into adults, I began keeping a journal of my personal prayer life. I wish I had known about keeping a prayer journal sooner. It would not have changed my prayers, but it would have enhanced them.

Keeping a prayer journal accomplishes two important things in my prayer life. First, it serves as a reminder of the consistency of my praying. I date my journal entries, so I know if I miss multiple days. Before I journaled, I had no record of the consistency of my prayer efforts. Please understand that I do not view prayer from a legalistic perspective; I do not feel guilty if I miss a day in my journal. I consider my prayer journal as a reminder, like a close friend who would remind me if we did not talk in several days. The journal produces a longing and a reminder to stay in touch, as I would with a phone call to a loved one or friend. The longing leads to an effort to communicate more frequently because I care.

Second, keeping a prayer journal allows me to document the things I am praying for. Through my journal, I have a tangible way to keep track of specific prayers, along with the answers and direction I receive from God. It provides a way to reflect back on what God has done through my prayers. Keeping a journal helps foster a heart and attitude of gratitude as I realize God's faithfulness to answer my prayers.

In Chapter 6 I shared the story of Lisa and the word God gave me for her to wait on her match-made-in-heaven. As a freshman in college, she developed a serious interest in a young man she was dating. Jan and I were concerned about the relationship, but we knew it was between Lisa and God.

One morning as I was praying, Lisa came to mind. I felt God speak to my heart. He said Lisa was okay, but He had a promise for her. Here is the entry from my journal:

January 22, 1996—As I was thinking and praying for Lisa, I felt the Lord put this impression on my heart for Lisa. The Lord said, "I am preparing a husband for Lisa, and he will fulfill all her desires, and he will love Me first—with all his heart. Tell her I am preparing a husband for her, and he will be everything she desires. Tell her not to compromise her desires in order to get a husband. I will provide her with one that will fulfill all her desires!"

A short time later, I called Lisa. As we talked, she told me she was trying to decide what to do with her relationship with this young man. I thought how timely was the word the Lord gave me! I told Lisa what God had spoken to me in my prayer time. There was no pressure on my part and no attempt to manipulate her with a spiritual message. I simply gave her an encouraging word from God spoken right to her heart. It was to encourage her faith at a critical point. It was her choice whether to receive the word as from God or not. She did take it as God's message to her, which lead her to re-evaluate her relationship with the young man she was dating. Shortly thereafter, the relationship ended.

During the next two years, Lisa occasionally said to me, "Dad, remind me what God said in the word about my husband." I would go back and reference my journal to recount to her exactly what I heard and wrote the day I received it in my prayer time. Two years went by. Lisa transferred to Baylor University in Waco, Texas, and she was home for the Thanksgiving holiday.

While she was home, a group of singles from the church came to our house to hang out and play games. A young man caught Lisa's eye that night. They spent quite a bit of time together before she went back to school. Through separate experiences, the Lord spoke to both Jan and me that this young man was the man He had prepared for Lisa. More than two years had passed since I received that word written in my journal, and it would involve another thirteen months of dating to complete the Lord's work in both of them before they married.

Partnering with God in His work in the development of our children is exciting. Prayer is the essential link that facilitates our partnership. There are many examples of prayer I could share. Just as no two children are the same, the prayer needs of each child are not the same either. Our connection with our children establishes an awareness of their individual needs, and our partnership with God removes the burden of absolute responsibility from us and transfers it to Him. His yoke is not too burdensome, nor is it too heavy to carry. He is able to change and affect things that I cannot touch, even by a Herculean human effort. *Prayer changes things*!

A Concluding Thought

I hope this chapter has encouraged you to partner with God through prayer in the development of your children. Partnering with God is not hard. Your personal worthiness has no bearing on it. Prayer is about communicating with Him to see His purposes accomplished in your children's lives. It is never too late to start, so don't worry if your kids are older or if you have lost some developmental years. Even if your children are now adults with children of their own, you can partner with God to see His purposes realized in every situation in your children and grandchildren.

The prayers of a father have great power to influence his children and future generations.

God is still on the throne, and prayer changes things!

18

Establishing Your Legacy

A financial inheritance is temporary,
but a godly heritage is eternal.

H ave you ever had investment regret? You know, the feeling that comes when you purchase something of great price and later realize that the cost wasn't worth the benefit you received. Life is a priceless, strategic investment, and we should intentionally focus on the legacy we are creating for future generations.

As a child, I remember listening to my parents comment on how fast time went by. I wondered, *Are they looking at the same clock I am?* Most often these comments were made around Christmas or during times of transition, such as birthdays or graduations. I am sure you too heard your parents commenting, perhaps with a twinge of regret, on how life had flown by, as if time had suddenly advanced from the day of your birth to your graduation day overnight. You probably thought, as I did, that this was crazy talk. If nothing else, time moves slowly and doesn't speed up for anyone or anything, right?

Well, I now have the same perspective that my parents did, one that comes from parenting and grand-parenting over many years. The very idea I thought was "crazy talk" is actually right! It is the perspective that recognizes how fast time passes when measured against the events of our lives and our life span. This happens partly, I think, because of our distraction and lack of attentiveness in the mundane moments of life. This is why it is so important to seize and savor every moment, even in life's seemingly insignificant situations. While perhaps plentiful in the present, our time, emotions, and resources will quickly be gone, never to be relived—only to be reviewed with celebration or regret.

The Big Question

What will be the legacy of your life? Have you ever thought about your legacy? Do you realize your legacy is being created right now? Most of us don't give it much thought, if any, until the second half of our lives. Why is this? I think it is at least in part due to the urgent demands of the "now" in the early seasons of life. Establishing a career, beginning a family, building a business, and nurturing a marriage all demand consider-able time and energy. By the time we finally have some margin in our lives in these areas, we find ourselves behind the "curve," struggling to make the necessary investments that will produce the legacy we desire.

As I explained in the introduction of this book, *legacy* is the all-encompassing term for what we will leave to our children and future generations. It includes both *inheritance* and *heritage*. Proverbs 13:22 tells us that a good man leaves an inheritance to his children's children. As good fathers, we all want to leave resources for our children and grandchildren that will enable them to start at a better place than we did when we began this life.

However, a financial inheritance is easily used up. The main foundation of our legacy must be a godly heritage that transfers our values, character, and beliefs to our children. Heritage includes the moral and spiritual underpinnings of our lives and reflects our devotion to God in how we speak and act in every situation. A financial inheritance is temporary, but a godly heritage is eternal.

> *Heritage includes the moral and spiritual underpinnings of our lives and reflects our devotion to God in how we speak and act in every situation.*

Legacy is not developed through a single event or a short-term investment of efforts to be moral or to develop a religious relationship with God. Legacy is built through many small, strategic investments of the living resources we have and steward over time. Each generation adds to the influence that becomes the legacy we leave and pass along to our children, grandchildren, and future generations.

Think of the legacy Billy Graham leaves for Ruth Graham Lutz and Franklin Graham or the legacy Martin Luther King left for his children, Martin Luther King III, Yolanda King, Dexter Scott King, and Bernice King. What an influence to draw from and what a platform to build the expression of their lives upon!

The legacy we leave to our children can be positive or negative, and it can be built upon with nurturing or destroyed through rejection or neglect. Either way, the reality is that our lives have powerful influence on the generations that follow us.

Two Secrets to Building Your Legacy

THE PRINCIPLE OF TRANSFERENCE

I have addressed the principle of transference throughout this book. Through the effective application of this principle, we build reputation, influence, qualities, and values that we transfer to our children and future generations. We can only transfer what we have experienced ourselves. We can only transfer as inheritance the physical resources that we own, and we can only transfer as heritage the character, values, and beliefs that we possess and express.

> *We can only transfer as inheritance*
> *the physical resources that we own,*
> *and we can only transfer as heritage*
> *the character, values, and beliefs that*
> *we possess and express.*

This principle applies to how God transfers resources to us. Fortunately, God is the owner of all the resources in the universe! There are many examples of God transferring resources to His people. Deuteronomy 4:19 describes all creation as a *heritage* He has given to everyone under heaven. Deuteronomy 33:4 describes the law as a *heritage* of the congregation of Jacob. Psalm 119:111 declares God has given us the *heritage* of the nations. Psalm 127 says children are a *heritage* from the Lord, and Psalm 136 describes the Promised Land as a *heritage* to Israel. Finally, Jeremiah provides this timeless and profound truth about the transference of God's *heritage*:

"But I said:

'How can I put you among the children
And give you a pleasant land,
A beautiful *heritage* of the hosts of nations?'

"And I said:

'You shall call Me, *My Father*,
And not turn away from Me'" (Jeremiah 3:19
emphasis added).

God's tool for the purpose of transference is the Holy
Spirit who transfers to us the principles and character of
God through His Word, His Church, and His indwelling.

THE PRINCIPLE OF COMPOUNDING

A second powerful secret to building a legacy is the
principle of compounding. It is through the cumulative
efforts of compounding investments of our finances,
time, qualities, character, and values that we build
influence, establish direction, and transfer a foundation
that influences future generations. The sooner we start,
the more dramatic the effect on our legacy.

Consider this well-known illustration of the principle
of financial compounding: If you have a penny and
double its value each day, how much would you have at
the end of one month? $1,000? $100,000? Would you
rather have a million dollars now or the value of that
penny after one month? Well, the fact is that the value
of a penny that doubles every day for 30 days would be
$5,368,709.12!

Here is the table showing the calculation:
The value in a 31-day month would be over $10 million!

The principle of compound growth is powerful. There are two lessons we should take from this principle. First, the rate of return is relevant. If I gave you a penny today, chances are that you would not grow it to $5 million in a month. Why? Because a 100% return on investment is almost impossible for anyone to achieve. More conservatively, if you invested the penny and doubled it every year for 30 years, how much money would you have? The same $5,368,709.12.

Second, time is more important than the rate of return. In this example, after 30 days you would have over $5 million; however, take away just three days, and on the 27th day you would have less than $1 million—on the 24th day less than $100,000.

Day	Value
1	$0.01
2	$0.02
3	$0.04
4	$0.08
5	$0.16
6	$0.32
7	$0.64
8	$1.28
9	$2.56
10	$5.12
11	$10.24
12	$20.48
13	$40.96
14	$81.92
15	$163.84
16	$327.68
17	$655.36
18	$1,310.72
19	$2,621.44
20	$5,242.88
21	$10,485.76
22	$20,971.52
23	$41,943.04
24	$83,886.08
25	$167,772.16
26	$335,544.32
27	$671,088.64
28	$1,342,177.28
29	$2,684,354.56
30	$5,368,709.12

Day	Value	Day	Value
1	$0.01	16	$327.68
2	$0.02	17	$655.36
3	$0.04	18	$1,310.72
4	$0.08	19	$2,621.44
5	$0.16	20	$5,242.88
6	$0.32	21	$10,485.76
7	$0.64	22	$20,971.52
8	$1.28	23	$41,943.04
9	$2.56	24	$83,886.08
10	$5.12	25	$167,772.16
11	$10.24	26	$335,544.32
12	$20.48	27	$671,088.64
13	$40.96	28	$1,342,177.28
14	$81.92	29	$2,684,354.56
15	$163.84	30	$5,368,709.12

Combining the awareness of the principle of transference with the concept of compounding challenges us to make the most of our resources—both finances and time.

DO YOU HAVE A PENNY?

Do you consider yourself wealthy? Are you working hard to amass assets to transfer to future generations? Regardless of the money you may have, I submit you are wealthier than you realize. The true measure of wealth goes far beyond the physical assets that will one day become our children's inheritance. There is nothing wrong with money, but remember, the Bible says, "The love of money is a root of all *kinds* of evil" (1 Timothy 6:10). True, lasting wealth consists of things such as our commitment to God, our relationships (especially church and family), our ethical behavior, and our life experiences. These are the important factors that become our heritage for future generations. Again, the value of our heritage far supersedes the financial resources we pass on as an inheritance.

Our legacy, then, is shaped primarily by the time and investment of those spiritual resources mentioned above. In several passages of Scripture, God promises to show love to "a thousand generations of those who love me and keep my commandments" (Deuteronomy 5:10; Exodus 20:6 NIV). Just like the return we expect on tangible assets, when we invest our time and effort into these *intangible* resources, God builds them into a lifetime of influence and impact upon others, which then becomes the key part of the legacy of our lives.

These investments are often small and may seem inconsequential at the time. However, God defines His own version of compounding in Scripture. First, He makes it clear that with only the smallest "mustard seed" faith, His children can achieve great things, which in this context means have great influence. God compounds this equivalent of a "penny" so that we can move mountains (Matthew 17:20). And it is truly God's work—read 1 Corinthians 3:1–10.

We are blessed that God has such a long memory. He promises to remember our faithfulness for a thousand generations! Of course, this also means our legacy is defined in the context of the contributions of those who came before us and, to some degree, those who come after us. Just like compound interest, the effects of the impact and influence of each generation are multiplied over time. Think of families you know who have a heritage of public service (the Kennedys); business expertise (the Rockefellers); and athletic achievement (the Mannings). The accomplishments in their respective areas were created over generations, in some cases from small beginnings. You may not be as well-known as these families, and your scope of influence and impact may seem smaller, but through transference and compounding over time, you can create a strategically-focused, godly heritage that will define a powerful legacy that God will use to bless many future generations.

The next question—where do you begin?

Define Your Values, Purpose, and Mission

The place to begin is a who, not a where. It is *you*. Are you living your life with purpose? Do you live your faith for others to see? Do you strive to have an intimate relationship with God, even against all the influences attempting to draw you in another direction? You can't live for yourself and expect to create influence that will become a multigenerational heritage that will help build an awesome family legacy.

If you haven't done this already, I suggest you define your values. Ask yourself if you consistently express your values in the decisions and actions of your life. *Make this your goal.* Then, do you know your purpose? Do you know the unique reason you were placed on this earth? Are you functioning in your purpose? Are your actions and activities moving you toward living out your purpose? *Make this your aim.* Finally, can you define your mission? Your mission is your purpose expressed in specific actions. *Make this your focus.*

DEFINE YOUR VALUES

What are your values? What lies at the root of the decisions you make? Is it feelings in the moment? Compassion? A desire for justice or fairness? A judgment or vow you previously made? As I considered these questions for myself, I realized my values were anchored in the absolute truth of God's Word. My actions weren't based on how I felt. After all, I know that my feelings are not to be trusted because they often stem from anger, hurt, frustration, or a desire for revenge. These feelings are not the best foundation for making decisions. Right and wrong, compassion, justice, and fairness are all anchored in an understanding of God's nature and character. God's

Word is real and true and unchanging. It is trust-worthy for every situation.

Back to the question. What are your values? What are they based upon? Do you know? Before you define your values, ask yourself what the values for your decisions and actions are based upon—feelings, circumstances, or an unchanging foundation of absolutes? Values that flow from feelings or circumstances are constantly shifting. Shifting values will not transfer well across multiple generations. Our heritage must be built on an unshifting foundation. This is why understanding the foundation on which our values rest is so important. Now we are ready to identify the values upon which we govern our lives and base our actions.

The place to start is with a pen and a journal. Using this "old school" method (or your computer or phone, if you prefer), list the actions or behaviors that you *do*—not ones you aspire to do but ones you actually do. Remember, you can only transfer to your children what you live for yourself. You don't have to be perfect, but there needs to be some fruit on your behavioral tree for actions to be placed on your list. Here are some examples to get you started:

- I have a daily morning quiet time.
- I prioritize going to church.
- I will be married to my wife for my whole life, no matter what, for better or for worse.

- I will tell the truth even when it hurts.
- I will not exaggerate the facts of a circumstance.
- I will be loyal to family and friends.
- I will not make money my god.
- I will work hard and provide a good life for my family.
- I will seek to be an example of godliness to others.
- I will enjoy the resources God gives me to steward.

As I wrote down my declarations, it wasn't long before I had a page full of actions and behaviors based on values with roots in my commitment to God and my ongoing relationship with Him. It is my goal to serve God with my whole heart and influence as many people as I can to do the same. My values point me toward my goal, and my actions reflect my mission. Yours will do the same for you.

List your actions and behaviors and be honest with yourself. Once you have a list, it will be easier for you to identify the values behind the items on your list. If you need to make a second list, do so. Make the second a list of actions and behaviors you don't do but want to start doing. This list will reveal values that are dormant and need your attention to be brought to life. Finally, a third list might be helpful. On this list identify all the actions and behaviors you have been doing but no longer want to be a part of your life. This will help you identify counterfeit values and habits that have developed from influences you don't want in your life. Using these lists, identify and clearly define the values that guide your decision making.

Although I had not written down my values before I started this process for myself, I quickly realized that my behavior and actions were focused toward a specific life purpose or mission. My life purpose has its roots in my commitment to God. I say "yes" and "no" to opportunities in my life based on this commitment, and I pursue passions that I think are part of God's work through my life.

I realized that in my parenting I had applied my values throughout my children's elementary and preteen years. I guided their lives with the same criteria I used for my own. It made sense because I wanted them to love God and follow Him just as I did. I could lead them to the decision, and I could model it for them, but ultimately it would be their choice to make before God. By defining the values and purpose behind my decision-making process, I clarified the "why" for myself so I could answer the same question when my children asked me.

DISCOVER YOUR PURPOSE

I gave my life to God when I was sixteen. As I matured into adulthood I realized my purpose was to represent God in every expression of my life and to follow His leading in all circumstances. As God's representative, I must strive to influence as many people as I can for Him and His kingdom. This clarity of purpose emerged as a reflection of my commitment and service to God. It has remained my focus through every season of life. I measure friendships, career advancement, business relationships, churches, and each opportunity for service by my purpose. This measuring is done naturally, organically, and in the background of all my thinking and decision making.

When I began the process of defining my values, purpose, and mission, I realized that I had subconsciously already done so. My purpose wasn't written down or clearly articulated, but it was evident in how I addressed opportunities big and small. As my purpose came into focus, a phrase developed as part of the expression of my life: "You are either an influence or you are being influenced." In his letter to the Corinthian church, Paul explains the truth behind this concept: "Bad company corrupts good morals" (1 Corinthians 15:33 NASB). I knew I did not want to be corrupted by bad influences—I wanted to *be* the influence for the people and situations of my life. This statement became my mantra, and I used it to remind myself of my purpose. As my children grew from infants to adults, I frequently spoke it to them as well. I wanted them to influence people for God and His kingdom.

*You are either an influence or you are
being influenced.*

DEVELOP YOUR MISSION

As my children moved into their teen years, I knew I
would begin making fewer and fewer of their decisions
directly. They were assuming more responsibility for
their choices, as well as the resulting consequences.
I could still help, though, by giving them the tools
they needed to make good decisions. One of the most
important tools was understanding the "why" behind
the decisions Jan and I had made for them over the
years. If our children knew the "why," they could use it
as a basis for their own decisions as they moved toward
adulthood.

My long list of actions and behaviors revealed without
a doubt that they expressed my values. I wanted to
streamline the list, but how? I realized that the actions
and behaviors fell into groupings that had to do with
purpose or mission. As I reviewed the list, I asked myself
questions such as "Why do I hold this value?" and "Why
do I do this particular thing?" This made the purpose
or mission behind each point come into clear focus. It
is similar to looking at a picture with no defined shape.
After first, it just appears like a bunch of multicolored
dots, but when you stare at it with strategic purpose,

a shape or picture appears. As I focused on my list of behaviors, these five larger statements came into view:

I want to influence as many people as I can for God and His kingdom.

This is the filter I use to decide about opportunities. It is why I say no to certain invitations. It's not that they are wrong, but they could negatively affect my influence.

I want to fulfill my marriage vows for a lifetime.

This is the reason I guard my heart. It is why I avoid compromising situations that might put my relationship with my wife at risk. It is why I say no to pornography and other lusts—because I want to fulfill my vows to Jan for a lifetime.

I will work hard to discover, embrace, and fulfill God's will for my life.

I believe God has a good plan for each person's life. I want to know and do His will with all my heart, mind, soul, and strength. I believe the best and most satisfying life is lived in devotion and service to God and others.

I will provide for my family, and we will enjoy the abundance that God liberally supplies.

God is the Creator and sustainer of all things. He knows, understands, and loves beauty better than anyone. He is not ashamed of excellence; in fact, excellence and beauty surround Him. I will keep Him first, and in so doing I will be free to enjoy all He has created and given to me.

I will serve God and people through active involvement in a local congregation of Christian believers.

The Church is God's bride, a collection of His people. The Church is not a building, but building are places where God's people meet and His work is done. God inhabits the praises of His people. I will not simply be an occasional attendee, but I will actively and consistently engage with my church in order to deepen my faith and to bless and build up the body of Christ.

Once you have defined your values, discovered your purpose, and developed your mission, there is one last thing to do: discuss them with your spouse and revise as needed so that they fully reflect you as a couple. Then, share everything with your children. This can be done in the form of a simple statement and question, such as:

These are the values and mission that have been behind the decisions your mom and I made for you until now. Do you want to have these values as your own as you move into adult living? If you see behavior or actions in me that don't line up with these values or mission, you can call me out. If you say you want to live by these, and I see behavior that is inconsistent with these values, I will call you out. If you don't want these values and mission as your own, then I would like you to tell me what your values and mission will be as you move into adult living.

We had these conversations with our children as they moved into their teenage years and as they prepared to leave home for college and adult living. As they approached marriage, we shared our values and mission with their fiancées. It served as both a final review for our children and an introduction and commitment for their fiancées to the values that guide our family. Through this process our family thrives in loving accountability and commitment to each other, and the succeeding generations will have a value map to navigate their lives. We want to do life in a supportive and loving partnership, and we work together to protect the influence and impact of our family's legacy.

Value Quality Time Together

The pace of life can be hectic, so we must be strategic in how we invest our time. In my family, there are two things that have become important investments of quality time. First, for more than 40 years, we have taken an annual family vacation together. It started when Jan and I got married. Her parents invited us to go with them on summer vacation, and every year since, with an ever-expanding footprint of family members, we have vacationed together. Jan's siblings and their spouses and children join in, and some summers have included my mom and sisters as well. As our individual families have grown and matured, we have maintained our time together. Parents, siblings, cousins, second cousins— all commit their time and resources to this annual gathering. Yes, is it crazy, loud, and takes coordination and commitment, but it is so worth it.

My favorite time is when we sit in the main cabin and sing, worship, share the events of the past year, and pray for each other. It is so very special, and I pray it never stops. Jan's dad has gone to be with the Lord, and her mom can no longer attend, but Jan and I, along with our siblings, have stepped up to carry on the tradition. Our children have also committed their vacation time and resources. It is an amazing time to be together, encourage one another, and celebrate God's work in each of us.

The second thing we do to prioritize our time together is what we call "Family Lunch" every Saturday. This is for in-town family as well as visiting family when they are with us. It involves a smaller number of people than summer vacation, but the group is still large—many weeks more than 30. This makes choosing the restaurant where we will meet a monumental task, but the effort is well worth it. Our lunch serves as a weekly check-in for everyone to share what is happening and how we can support and help each other. It is a special time.

Time is a gift we must choose to invest. We recognize that everyone is busy with many demands, so making these investments of time is not taken for granted. Family feuds cannot be allowed to exist. Coping mechanisms like denial or avoidance only lead to bigger problems with devastating results. If there is an offense or frustration, it must be proactively talked and worked through. We must allow our love for one another to be greater than any idiosyncrasies or flaws.

How are you investing your time? Maybe it can't be with your extended family like we have done. What about with your children and grandchildren? We have found that it helps new and growing families to participate if we offer to cover some or all of the expense. It is part of the commitment and sacrifice involved in building your heritage and nurturing the legacy you desire.

I recommend you establish some special events for your family. If possible, start when your children are young and in your home. Make it a priority for all to participate, and make exceptions rare. You will notice as times goes by that your family stories and memories will be built around things that happened in these special family events. Use them as strategic opportunities to impart and reinforce you values, purpose, and mission.

Provide Positive Validation and Support

The apostle Paul writes that the kingdom of God is "righteousness, peace, and joy in the Holy Spirit" (Romans 14:17 NIV). God believes in encouragement and celebration, and so do we in the Lane family. We love one another, and nothing is better than celebrating an accomplishment, family addition, or birthday. We love being together, and we try to support each other as often as we can in the activities of our lives. We make a diligent commitment to be present and acknowledge weddings, graduations, and special times for each other. It is not a legalistic requirement but a heart desire to share in each other's joys and accomplishments. This is also true in the hard seasons of life—through sickness, job change or loss, marriage difficulty, or something impacting our children or grandchildren. We pray for, encourage, love, and support each other through the tearful seasons of life just as much as the exciting, joyful seasons. It is part of our heritage.

A Final Thought

Legacy relates to the future, and the future may seem so far off. Don't be distracted, though; the future will arrive faster than we expect. You may feel that you are too busy in the moment to consider building for the future. The present has its own demands that can feel so critical that it seems necessary, even prudent at times, to focus solely on them. We may put off the thought of the heritage we are building and the legacy it reflects.

Perhaps it seems a little morbid to think in these futuristic terms. It may even feel self-serving to think about strategically building your legacy when you are young, as though you are being presumptuous. Don't be overcome or distracted; instead, be encouraged and inspired to build something great that is transferred as a heritage for your life and family.

Don't avoid your legacy. Realize that to think about it and plan for it is not morbid but wise, thoughtful, and loving. It is the godliest thing we can do and serves as our guard against future regret. It paves the way for us to hear, "Well done good and faithful servant!" as we enter into eternity with the One who matters most—our Lord and Savior, Jesus Christ!

Study Guide

How to Use the Study Guide

T his Study Guide can be utilized for group study or
individual reflection. It is divided into sections and
designed for participants to engage in after reading the
corresponding chapters of the book. Each Study Guide
section contains the following components:

RECAP

A brief overview of the material in the chapters.

GROUP OPENER

Icebreaker questions to talk through and share.

DISCUSS

Questions for discussion.

PRAY/HEAR

A time for personal reflection and communication with God.

DIG DEEPER

Exercises to help individuals further process what was discussed at the group meeting and what God spoke.

REMEMBER

Key points or takeaways from the chapters.

Study Guide

Introduction and Chapter 1

RECAP

Whether you are a father, want to be a father, or just have a father, there is so much to be learned from our heavenly Father on this subject.

You may be thinking that you didn't have a good relationship with your dad; "I don't know how to parent children." Or perhaps you had a *great* dad; "I know all about this parenting thing!" Maybe your children are grown, and you're convinced there's nothing left to do. God, our perfect Father, has things to say to you—to all of us.

Never underestimate your influence as a father. People's view of God is directly correlated to their experiences with their own fathers. You have a *direct influence* on the spiritual lives of your children. This influence has a ripple effect across future generations.

God is the Creator and owner of all things, and we are responsible to Him for our actions.

GROUP OPENER

If you have children, briefly describe one of your favorite "dad-moments" with them. How do you think this moment impacted your children? If you don't have children, briefly recall one of your favorite moments with your own father. How did this moment impact you?

DISCUSS

- What are some of your goals as a father?
- What is the principle of transference?
- Read Psalm 139. According to this passage, what kind of father is God? List some of His characteristics.
- What characteristics does God seek to transfer to us as His children?
- How have the men in your life viewed God? Did they see following Him as a sign of weakness or strength? How have their views shaped yours?
- In order to pass along these values to our children, we must have a relationship with God ourselves. Where are you in this process? Is God simply a religious concept? Or have you come to know Him personally? If you are not sure, re-read the last part of Chapter 1, taking time to pray and ask God where you stand with Him.

PRAY/HEAR

Talking about fathers and fathering may bring up some painful wounds from your past. Maybe your father wasn't a good father; maybe he was absent; maybe he was abusive. Whatever your experience with your earthly father, God wants to heal those hurt places and show you what a good, kind, and loving Father He is.

You may need to admit to yourself that your father's choices hurt you. As men, we often think that to admit pain is to admit weakness; however, God cannot heal what you will not share with Him. Take a minute and ask Him: *Lord, what hurts am I carrying as a result of my father's choices?*

DIG DEEPER

Search for the characteristics of God in each of the following passages:

- John 6:45
- Acts 2:33
- Romans 1:7
- Romans 8:15
- Galatians 1:4
- Ephesians 1:17
- 1 Thessalonians 3:13
- Hebrews 12:7

As you begin your journey through this study, ask God to show you who He is as a Father.

REMEMBER

- Children are a gift from God (see Psalm 127:3).
- What we model and transfer to our children through our behavior must be a reflection of God and His plans for our life and theirs.
- We will only transfer to our children the values and character demonstrated in our own lives.
- There are two foundational truths that should radically shape our view of the parenting:
- God is the Creator and owner of all things.
- We are responsible to Him for our actions.
- We must have a personal relationship with God to be able to transfer it to our children.

Study Guide

Chapters 2-4

RECAP

W hile the Bible clearly states in Psalm 127 that children are a gift from the Lord, it also tells us in Proverbs that there is foolishness in the heart of every child. Our responsibility as fathers is to identify the foolishness and correct it by aiming our children in a direction of connection with the Lord.

How do we do this? First of all, we must understand the difference between *foolishness* and *childishness*. As parents, we walk a fine line between helping our children drive out what doesn't belong and punishing them for something that they can't help.

Second, as we model and grow in our own understanding of godly principles, we transfer those precepts to our children and ask them to follow in our footsteps.

Third, we must instill a healthy fear of the Lord. Proverbs 9:10 tells us, "The fear of the Lord *is* the beginning of wisdom." Since our primary goal is to launch our children into the world with wisdom, we must understand what "the fear of the Lord" really means.

Setting these parameters in place provides the framework for instilling our values in our children from a place of godliness and integrity.

GROUP OPENER

Describe a time from your childhood when you behaved foolishly. How did your father respond? How did you respond?

DISCUSS

- What does *foolishness* mean? Define it in your own terms.
- According to this book, what might cause foolishness in children? What does the Bible say will get rid of foolishness in a child's heart?
- Who was the primary disciplinarian in your house when you were a child?
- Who is the primary disciplinarian in your house now? What does the Bible say about the role of a father in the house?
- Read and discuss Ephesians 6:4. What does it mean to "provoke" someone? What instruction does the verse give regarding fathers?

- Earlier in this study, we introduced the idea of "transference." What am you trying to transfer to your children?

PRAY/HEAR

Ask God these questions and listen for His response.

God, am I being a good example for my children? Has my character been consistent with the principles I am trying to teach them? Is there any area where I have allowed inconsistencies to creep in?

Father, have I been afraid to come to You? In what ways did my father show me an inaccurate view of You? Today, I choose to forgive my father for those things. Please show me the truth about You and how You treat me as a son.

God, would you show me what fun looks like?

DIG DEEPER

We can only transfer what we have. In light of this truth, take a moment and examine whether or not you truly have the things you are trying to transfer to your children.

Look for teaching moments—opportunities to discuss godly principles with your children. Also, look for ways to show your children how fun God really is!

Allow God to father you too. Allow Him to use teaching moments in your life.

REMEMBER

- A successful father is one who is able to correct foolish behavior without inflicting emotional hurt.
- We can only transfer what we have.
- Our children are influenced more by the life we model for them than by what we say, our good intentions, or any other factor of influence.
- Our children's view of God is directly shaped by their interactions with us.
- Every day is full of teaching moments with our children.
- Do not link acceptance of your children with their performance. They must know that they are always accepted, regardless of their behavior.

Study Guide

Chapters 5-6

RECAP

We must intentionally guide and shape our children's journey toward becoming men and women of character, accurately representing God to the world around them.

We know integrity is important. But how do we get it? It doesn't just happen. Galatians 5:22–23 lays out the fruit of the Spirit—things that should be visible results of an ongoing relationship with the Holy Spirit. The final fruit in the list is self-control.

How do we teach self-control? We teach principles intentionally and by example. The first thing we need to do as fathers is to examine our ability to manage ourselves. How do we handle different situations? Do we take responsibility for our actions, or do we cast blame on others? Are we in control of our emotional and spiritual health, or are we easily angered and swayed?

Men of character respond to the world around them, not the other way around. Men of integrity recognize that mistakes are inevitable, and they strive to take responsibility for their actions. Godly fathers walk in a spirit of self-control and teach their children to do the same.

GROUP OPENER

Consider the story I recalled about my lawn-mowing experience when I was 13 years old. Describe a similar experience from your own life. How did your parents handle it? How did you handle it?

DISCUSS

- Read Galatians 5:16–25. What *works of the flesh* stand out to you? Are there any that you struggle with or have struggled with?
- Look at the fruit of the Spirit listed in verses 22–23. What does *self-control* mean? How does it affect the other fruits listed?
- Is the fruit of self-control evident in your life? How do you respond when you or others make a mistake?
- Read Genesis 3. Adam and Eve had a choice in the garden of Eden. What did Adam and Eve freely choose? What were the consequences of their actions?

- Describe a time when you were allowed to fully experience the consequences of your actions. What did you learn from that experience?
- Describe a time when you had a choice to exercise self-control. What did you choose? If this experience was less than your best, how could you have chosen differently?

PRAY/HEAR

Read the list of the fruit of the Spirit. Which fruit do you want? The Bible says that we have not because we ask not (James 4:2). Ask God for it; He will give it to you.

Lord, I confess that at times I have chosen to blame others for my mistakes. I confess that I have not always been willing to accept responsibility for my own actions. I am sorry. Please forgive me! Lord, today I choose to be responsible for my own actions. I choose to exert self-control and manage my own choices and consequences. I choose today to be a man of integrity, a man of my word—just like You.

DIG DEEPER

Recognize that self-control does not mean *controlling*. It simply means that you will be in control of *you*, no matter what anyone else does. As a parent, this can sometimes be difficult. Pay close attention to your responses to others this week. Are you in control of you? Is the fruit of the Spirit evident in your life, no matter what your circumstances are?

REMEMBER

- Self-control is a fruit of the Spirit.
- Integrity and character are results of self-control.
- Integrity and character are present when our words and our actions line up.
- As a father, it is your role to point your children to the character of God.

Study Guide

Chapters 7-10

RECAP

Discipline can be a scary word for many people. It can bring up painful memories of the misuse of disciplinary methods or even downright abuse. Remember, this is not at all what God intended when He designed parents and children.

Discipline, according to God's methods, is not punishment. It is not revenge or control; in fact, truly godly discipline is meant for the exact opposite. It is meant to provide guidance and responsibility.

God's discipline is always redemptive. It always flows out of love and is meant to restore connection. Sin is what breaks our connection with God. Discipline is meant to reconnect us with Him, who loves us no matter what we do. God's discipline reflects His love for us. As parents, we are responsible to reflect God's nature to our children—even when they mess up.

The three key components of discipline are submission, correction, and accountability. As parents, we should never discipline out of anger, frustration, embarrassment, pride, or inconvenience. Such discipline will only end up harming our children rather than helping them.

GROUP OPENER

What disciplinary methods were used in your house growing up? Were they effective? Why or why not?

DISCUSS

- Define *submission*. How does submission look in your everyday life?
- The purpose of discipline is to maintain and/or restore connection. How is this different than how you may have looked at discipline in the past?
- Read 1 John 1:9. What does God require of us when we sin? What is our part, and what is His?
- Read Psalm 103:12. According to this verse, how should we handle our children's mistakes once they have asked forgiveness?
- Define *accountability*. What are some reasons men might resist the accountability that mentoring provides?

- Describe some characteristics of a good mentor. How do these compare with the characteristics of a good father?

PRAY/HEAR

Disciplining out of a wrong heart can lead to what we call judgments and inner vows.

A *judgment* is a negative statement against something: "My father is angry and yells at me. Therefore, all men are angry." An *inner vow* is a response to a judgment we have made: "Because all men are angry, I will never trust a man again." In the case of a harsh or abusive father, it can lead to judgments and inner vows that will prevent us from parenting our children in a healthy way. It can lead to abusive or controlling parenting or, on the other end of the scale, passivity resulting from an unwillingness to reenact what was modeled for us.

Neither method is healthy, so we need to deal with the judgments and inner vows we have made.

Ask: *Lord, what judgments have I made against You? Against others? What inner vows have I made as a result of these judgments? Lord, what is the truth about these things?*

Confess: *Yes, Lord. You're right. I did make these judgments and inner vows in my heart. I am sorry! Please forgive me.*

Choose to agree with the truth as He shows it to you.

DIG DEEPER

Describe your ideal relationship with your children. What choices can you make to create an environment where this relationship is possible?

You may discover during this process that you need to repent to your children for some things. Discuss these things with the Lord and act as He directs you.

If you don't have a mentor in your life, pray about who to ask. Ask that person to consider it. Purpose in your heart to be fully accountable—to be submitted, teachable, and correctable.

REMEMBER

- Submission is necessary for healthy relationships.
- Discipline must always come from a heart of love, compassion, and restoration.
- True accountability is necessary for growth.
- God causes all things to work together for the good of those who love Him!

Chapters 11-15

RECAP

S pending time with your children is crucial to developing a relationship with them.

Many men spend time together and enjoy things
with their friends to develop intimacy and connection;
however, many fathers don't view their children with the
same perspective. They think their children will grow
themselves up or that their wives can handle such things.

If this sounds ridiculous, statistics show that men are
less likely to engage with their children than their wives
are, and many men spend just a few minutes per day
with their children. If so, who is fathering them? Who is
identifying, supporting, and guiding the unique destiny
in each of them?

Teenagers present their own special set of parenting
challenges. As teenagers, our children walk a fine line
between childhood and adulthood. Physical, social, and
emotional changes happen at a rapid-fire pace. This time

for a young person can be one of growth and discovery with healthy boundaries and freedom, or it can be a time of anger, pain, and desolation. You, as a father, can be a catalyst for growth during this normally turbulent time.

GROUP OPENER

Describe your favorite memory from your teenage years.

DISCUSS

- What do you think when you hear the word "teenagers"? How do you respond when you see them?
- How does parenting change as your children approach adulthood? What challenges may emerge during the teenage years?
- How do your children see your relationship with God? Do they see you in close talks with Him about your destiny?
- What experiences can you provide for your children to help them discover their unique purpose?
- Describe you parenting relationship with your spouse. How is she similar to you? How is she different from you?
- What can you and your spouse do together to transfer your values to your teenager?

PRAY/HEAR

God is a kind, loving, all-present Father, always ready to listen, to talk, to be with us. Do you believe in your heart that God is interested in you and wants to be with you? We transfer our beliefs to our children—what beliefs are you transferring? Remember, a belief is not just a thought. Examine what you truly believe about God. Ask Him these questions:

God, what do I believe about You?

God, would You show me right now just how close You are?

God, do You want to spend time with me?

How do You feel about me?

DIG DEEPER

If you are married, read Chapter 12 together with your spouse. Discuss how you can better support each other in your parenting.

If you are divorced, and if it is possible, discuss this topic with your ex-spouse. Resolve to put aside animosity and hurts as you communicate with your children's mother.

Examine your own influence on your children. Are you stewarding it well, or are there some areas that need attention? Ask God to speak to you about these things.

REMEMBER

- It is crucial for fathers to spend time with their children.
- The mother of your children is your partner—and you are hers—in parenting your children.
- God has created all of us with a unique destiny and purpose.
- Teenagers need their dad too!

Study Guide

Chapters 16-17

RECAP

S ometimes children return after leaving the nest. There
are numerous reasons for this, such as job loss, divorce,
health, and economic issues, to name a few. For many
parents, this represents a new set of questions. How do we
parent an adult? Do they still need us? How involved—or
uninvolved—should we be? If their reasons for returning
involve problems and bad decisions, what then? Do we even
let them back in? How much do we support them?

Parenting never stops. Our children always need
our strength and encouragement, no matter their age
or situation. However, our role changes, as should our
methods.

The story of the prodigal son is a powerful example of
how to deal with these issues.

Regardless of the relationship, the commitment
to prayer is an essential factor in our parental role.
Parenting is, simply put, a partnership with God. It must

be a constant conversation with a God who has their best interest in mind and sees the end from the beginning—even when we can't.

Without prayer, we will inevitably lean on our own understanding, which the Bible warns against. We need to spend time in God's presence, talking and listening—praying with Him.

Even if you have been raised, like many men, to believe that you can "do it all yourself," the truth is that we as believers are designed to be plugged into the One who made us and loves us perfectly. This is never truer than when we take on the enormous responsibility of raising children.

GROUP OPENER

Describe your current relationship with your own parents. Are you close? In what ways are they still involved in your life?

DISCUSS

- What is the biblical definition of *inheritance*? How does this definition compare to our modern definition?
- How do you respond to your children's search for significance? How do you respond if and when they fail?

- What is the difference between *empowering* and *enabling*? How might the story of the prodigal son have turned out if the father had enabled his son?
- How have you responded when your children have made mistakes? How can you create a safe environment in which they can fail without fear of your response?
- According to the text, what is the definition of *prayer*? How does this compare to your understanding of it?
- Why do we need to pray? Do you see God as in control, meaning He will just do whatever He wants? Or do you view Him as a Father who is interested in the day-to-day details of His children? Describe how you see Him and how this shapes how you pray.

PRAY/HEAR

Talk to God. Converse. Relate. Come close.

Consider Moses—do you think that God wants to talk with you the same way He did with Moses?

Ask: *God, what would You like to talk about today?*

Take some time to talk to your heavenly Father. He wants to hear from you. If you haven't already done so, consider starting a prayer journal. Use it to record your prayers for your children and God's responses to you. Be sure to record answered prayers!

DIG DEEPER

Examine your relationship with your grown children. Have you purposely empowered them in their search for significance? Are there any ways in which you may have attempted to control or manipulate them? If and when they have failed, have you communicated shame or rejection in any way?

If your children are still at home, examine your current relationship with them. Are you empowering them at their current stage of exploration? What steps have you taken to ensure a safe place to fail and make mistakes?

Read Psalm 139 again. What does this chapter say about God's opinions and thoughts toward you?

REMEMBER

- A father's primary responsibility is to reveal God to his children by teaching them about Him and His ways.
- We cannot project our dreams and goals onto our children. We must allow them to discover their own uniqueness in Christ.
- True significance can only be identified in connection with God.
- We should empower our children's search for significance without enabling them in an unhealthy way.

- Prayer is crucial to parenting! We must partner with God.
- God will uphold His end of the partnership—always.

Chapter 18

RECAP

M any of us have never considered what the legacy of our lives will be. Although we don't usually think so when we are young, time passes quickly when measured against the events of our lives and our life span. This is why it is so important to seize and savor every moment and to wisely invest the time we have with our children.

What will your legacy be? What will future generations inherit and what heritage will they receive? Remember, a financial inheritance is easily used up. The main foundation of our legacy must be a godly heritage that transfers our values, character, and beliefs to our children. *A financial inheritance is temporary, but a godly heritage is eternal.*

The principles of transference and compounding are two powerful secrets to understand in order to help build your legacy—both inheritance and heritage.

To begin on the road to building this legacy, it is important to first define your values, your purpose, and your mission. Once you have done so, it is important to discuss and agree on these with your spouse, so that you can consistently transmit them to your children and monitor how they develop these principles as they mature.

Two final concepts are important to help in this family development. First, make every effort to enjoy quality family time together on a regular basis. Second, do everything possible to provide validation and support of each other, such as celebrating both the accomplishments and joys of life as well as the tough seasons.

Don't be distracted in building your family's legacy by all the busy-ness of life. Time is limited, but sharing time is the godliest thing you can do for your family.

GROUP OPENER

Growing up, do you remember having family discussions about tradition, history, and values? What did this look like?

DISCUSS

- What is the difference between inheritance and heritage?

- Discuss briefly the principles of transference and compounding. How do they apply to the concept of legacy?
- What are some of your values? Are there areas where your actions don't line up with your values?
- How would you describe your purpose?
- How would you state your mission?
- What are some ways you engage (or could engage) in family time together?

PRAY/HEAR

Look up verses that refer to *heritage*. (You can search on Bible Gateway, especially in the NKJV, NIV, and NASB versions.) What is God saying to you when you see these many examples and definitions of heritage?

Pray: *God, what do You want the legacy of my family to look like? Help me identify what I need to transfer to my children and how to communicate these things to them through my actions as well as my words. May my values, purpose, and mission be completely aligned with Your Word and Your will.*

DIG DEEPER

Look closely at the way you communicate values to your children. Consider carefully if your actions match up with your expressed values. If not, determine how to change that.

Read 1 Corinthians 3:1–10. How does this passage help you put in perspective your role to "plant" and "water" the seeds of godliness? What does it mean that God "gives the increase"?

Take time to examine yourself in light of what you have read and discussed over the course of this study. What kind of heritage do you want to transfer to your children? What steps will you take to do this? Start by writing down your values, purpose, and mission and discussing them with your wife (or your children's mother); agree on a plan to transmit these principles to your children.

REMEMBER

- You only have so much time to help develop your family heritage and contribute to your legacy.
- Heritage is far more important than physical possessions.
- Define your values, purpose, and mission, and use quality family time to reinforce them in your children.
- Celebrate, support, and build each other up.
- Don't be distracted by the demands of life from doing whatever is necessary to build your family legacy. It is the godliest thing you can do.

About the Author

Tom Lane has served in various capacities at Gateway Church since 2004. His most recent assignment was campus pastor of the Dallas campus, launched in 2016. There, he led the ministry team in executing the vision and values of Gateway as they ministered to the Dallas congregation.

Currently, Tom serves as the Apostolic Senior Pastor over the apostolic outreach ministries of the church. In this position, he oversees the outside ministries associated with Gateway Church and works directly with the Gateway Network team and the Gateway Business Leaders ministry.

Tom's ministry experience spans more than 35 years. His relational style and personal experiences bring a warmth to his leadership, speaking, writing, and pastoral ministry. In addition to his most recent book, *Tested and Approved,* he coauthored *He Still Speaks* with his friend, Wayne Drain, and *Strong Women and the Men Who Love Them* with his wife, Jan. Tom has also authored other books: *Foundations of Healthy Church Government, Tested and Approved Mentor Playbook, Conversations with God* and *Letters from a Dad to a Graduate.*

Tom and Jan have been married for more than 40 years and have four married children and 15 grandchildren.